I Gave

DATING

a

CHANCE

A Biblical Perspective
to Balance the Extremes

I Gave

DATING

a

CHANCE

Jeramy Clark

WATERBROOK
PRESS

I GAVE DATING A CHANCE
PUBLISHED BY WATERBROOK PRESS
12265 Oracle Boulevard, Suite 200
Colorado Springs, Colorado 80921
A division of Random House, Inc.

All scripture quotations, unless otherwise indicated, are taken from the
Holy Bible, New International Version®. NIV®. Copyright © 1973, 1978, 1984
by International Bible Society. Used by permission of Zondervan Publishing
House. All rights reserved. Lowercase pronouns for deity have been maintained
in quotations from the NIV in observance of copyright law. Also quoted is
The Message. Copyright © by Eugene H. Peterson 1993, 1994, 1995. Used by
permission of NavPress Publishing Group.

ISBN 978-1-57856-329-6

Copyright © 2000 by Jeramy Clark
Library of Congress Cataloging-in-Publication Data
Clark, Jeramy.
    I gave dating a chance : a biblical perspective to balance the extremes /
Jeramy Clark.
        p. cm.
    ISBN 1-57856-329-1
    1. Dating (Social customs) 2. Dating (Social customs)—Religious
aspects—Christianity.   I. Title.
HQ801.C56 2000
306.73'4—dc21   99-059022

Published in the United States by WaterBrook Multnomah, an imprint of the Crown
Publishing Group, a division of Random House Inc., New York.

Printed in the United States of America
2009

20   19   18   17   16   15   14   13   12

To my parents,

Spencer and Rona Clark.

Your faith taught me to believe

and your love told me I could do anything.

I love you.

And to my wife's parents,

J.A.C. and LeAnn Redford,

who model a passionate and transparent love.

Contents

To Date or Not to Date

I KNOW WHAT YOU'RE THINKING...

I'll bet I can guess one of the biggest issues in your life right now—maybe THE biggest. In fact, if all your thoughts from last week were recorded and labeled by topic (that's a scary thought!), your relationships with the opposite sex probably outweigh family, friends, school, job, and pretty much everything else.

I'd also guess that your thoughts on this subject are downright confusing. As a young Christian, you're faced with such conflicting opinions: Date. Don't date. Wait to date. Your head is probably spinning from all the advice.

WHY THIS BOOK?

I've been working with young adults for almost ten years now, including four years with nearly five hundred high-school students at the First Evangelical Free Church of Fullerton, California. At each place I've ministered, dating dilemmas have arisen constantly. Everywhere I've been—California, Washington, Arizona, Colorado, even overseas—young Christians have the same questions and concerns, the same ones I had and that you probably have.

These years of ministry to dating-age Christians have taught me that young people clearly want to date. But does merely having a desire to date make it okay to date?

No way!

On the other hand, I believe that learning to date according to God's standards *does* make it okay to desire and pursue relationships. I'm convinced that for young adults who love the Lord and who long to please Him, dating truly is an option. Young Christians *can* enjoy godly relationships if they approach dating with God's perspective and guidelines. Believers *can* get to know one another by responding to romantic feelings appropriately. God enables us to maintain healthy emotional, physical, and spiritual boundaries when we walk in step with the Holy Spirit.

What Should You Do?

Whether you've dated quite a bit or not at all, if you want to please God and to make sure you're headed in the right direction on the issue of dating, you've come to the right place. If your mind and heart have ever cried, "Lord, what do I do with this desire to date?" then this book is for you.

Maybe you're eager to date, but you've heard Christians shouldn't. After all, *dating* has become a dirty word in many Christian circles. Some recommend throwing out the whole idea. Maybe you've even tried not dating because you felt it was the godly thing to do. Perhaps you're now frustrated because not dating didn't solve your problems or address your concerns.

Even if you've never dated before, you may still feel torn between your heart's desire to date and the movement to ditch dating altogether.

While I wholeheartedly believe Christians need to clean up their dating act, I don't believe you have to reject dating to be godly in your relationships.

Of course discovering God's plan for your dating life may indeed mean that now is not the right time to date. There are seasons of life when dating isn't the best option. Because of higher priorities God has for you, you may not have time for a dating relationship. Or perhaps you've been hurt in a relationship and need some time to heal. Or it could be that you're too young and simply need to wait a little longer.

Don't worry if you're not sure about the timing issue. Later in the book, we'll look closer at recognizing the right time to date. Meanwhile, remember this: You don't have to keep struggling with unanswered questions about dating. As we'll see, the Bible can guide you through dating, step by step.

Whether or not you choose to date right now, I want you to have a biblical strategy for dating. I want your parents to trust you, your peers to respect you, and most of all for you to trust God's leading as you date.

MY STORY

Another reason I've written this book is simply my own story. It's easy for me to identify with whatever confusion you may be experiencing about dating. I remember when so many well-meaning friends filled my ears with dos and don'ts about dating. They made promises of happiness, success, and purity if I followed their suggestions. But often I wound up bewildered and frustrated.

Over time I experienced all kinds of dating ups and downs. Early on, while still in my teens, I tried the "world's way," playing games and playing the field. Not only did that leave me unsatisfied and often hurt, but it definitely didn't please God.

As I grew closer to the Lord, I truly wanted to please Him with every aspect of my life. I even went through a time of not dating in order to focus on the Lord more intently. He worked in me deeply during that time, building my character and showing me how to have good relationships. Though I wasn't dating, I was doing a lot of watching and wondering. I wondered if I'd ever find The One, and how I'd know she was it. I wondered if I could date to God's glory.

I found that I could. Through all the ups and downs, I believe God laid on my heart certain principles about dating that helped me to glorify Him in my relationships. After some years of experience, I knew God's standards better and how to put His truths into practice—although I've by no means mastered this process.

Meanwhile, in my youth ministry at Fullerton, I met a volunteer leader named Jerusha Redford. We began dating, and God helped me date Jerusha to His glory. It was awesome! Eventually Jerusha and I were married, just over a year ago.

I can see now how God used each of my dating experiences to make me ready for my wife. The principles of love I learned from God while dating are now a solid foundation for our marriage. I found out how to communicate, how to control my desires, how to be committed, and above all, how to concentrate on being right with God.

I want to share with you the guidelines I've learned from both successes and failures in my own dating life, as well as from the experiences of others I've associated with in ministry. I trust that these guidelines will help you develop healthy, enjoyable relationships as you apply God's timeless truth to your life.

GO TO THE SOURCE

Dating doesn't have to be confusing and frustrating—or worse, impossible.

Why not?

Because we have direct access to the Source—the Source of all answers and the Source of all fulfillment.

God is that ultimate Source. He has a lot to say about your relationships with the opposite sex. He's written a letter to you that's full of the best advice on love and relationships. You know it; it's the Bible.

The word *dating* might not appear in your Bible's concordance, but God's Word speaks loud and clear about all relationships. We'll look together at tons of examples and principles from the Bible that can guide us in our relationships and help us unravel the mystery of dating.

God's Word is relevant to every aspect of your life. By studying His Word you'll gain not only great dating advice, but so much more. Listen to this:

> The statutes of the LORD are trustworthy,
>> making wise the simple.
> The precepts of the LORD are right,
>> giving joy to the heart.
> The commands of the LORD are radiant,
>> giving light to the eyes. (Psalm 19:7-8)

This passage promises three amazing results of searching God's Word. Look at the passage again. Do you see all three?

When we apply His timeless truths to our dating life, we find...

- WISDOM. Do you want to be a "smart date"? Do you want to know how to act and speak? God's Word will make you wise.
- JOY! Dating can be fun, and I firmly believe it can be a wonderful time of growth as well. As you follow God's lead and His righteous ways, you will have joy in dating.
- LIGHT. That means you'll have direction. You can see where you're going. You won't feel blind or abandoned but will be guided by the Good Shepherd Himself.

Incredible promises, aren't they? And they're yours for the taking! If you're willing and ready to pursue God's truth, this book can help you experience dating in an ultimately satisfying way that brings glory to God.

So...enough with intros. Let's get down to business!

The Drive to Date

Nature, Love, and Especially God

———

"The tragedy of our age," my wife once heard a pastor say, "is that we're at a crossroads, but all the signposts have fallen down."

You're at a crossroads when it comes to dating. That's why you're reading this book. You're a Christian who wants to serve the Lord and understand His will. You want to keep your dating life under His control. But you've probably been confused by all the fallen signposts around you.

The world's way of dating definitely doesn't suit you. It's full of mind games and usually ends in heartache and burned bridges. You can't follow those directions.

No wonder a whole movement against Christian dating has gained popularity. Some Christians say that since romantic feelings can lead to sin, the only godly course for young people is not to date. "Courtship" is acceptable, they say, but only when a person is ready for marriage. In their eyes, casual one-on-one dating will only distract young people from their walks with the Lord.

These Christians who discourage dating have good motives, and their goal—to keep young adults pure—is a great one. But their approach, I believe, is imbalanced. I believe we *can* apply the Lord's truth to our romantic relationships as we date. We *can* find a workable strategy for dating and getting to know others, all to God's glory.

Can you please the Lord and still date? I'll answer that question with an emphatic yes! There *is* a godly alternative to "kissing dating good-bye."

IT'S A NATURAL THING

562-694-26…Click.

C'mon! I can do this.

562-694-266…Click.

Darn it. I'm twenty-six years old. Why am I still sweaty-palmed and freaked-out that her dad will answer?

But if her dad does answer, I can't risk the possibility of Star 69 or Caller ID. I'll just have to ask if I can talk to her.

You may laugh, but this really happened to me. And it wasn't that long ago, when I was trying to make a call to the woman who's now my wife.

Did I finally get through all ten digits of her phone number? Yes, and you'll never guess one of the reasons why: a TV commercial, of all things.

An old man and his grandson were sitting on a porch swing. The grandpa asked if his grandson ever intended to get married. The young boy reacted as most boys his age would, with horror and complete disgust. He thought falling in love was about as unnatural as eating broccoli.

Luckily his porch-swing partner knew better. "Falling in love," the grandfather said, "is the most natural thing in the world."

That bit of wisdom reassured me I wasn't crazy for wanting to get to know someone special. It was natural to feel the way I did, to have that aching desire in my heart to spend the rest of my life with someone, to feel unsatisfied with being on my own, to really want to find the right person.

Don't get me wrong; I wasn't desperate, and I felt content in my relationship with God. I just had this drive in me that wouldn't let me alone.

I wanted to fall in love—"the most natural thing in the world." Think about it.

THE DRIVE TO DATE

I didn't care much for science until my sophomore year of high school, when I had biology with Mr. Carlson. A six-foot-six all-star athlete, he would literally walk on top of our lab tables and randomly thwack desks with his lecture stick to keep our attention.

He sure kept mine. Under Mr. Carlson's teaching, I became fascinated by the details of all life forms, from plants to pigs. Ever since then, I've loved and appreciated the natural order in God's creation. Things make sense, and life follows patterns that we can study.

There's even a pattern for the development of a drive to date.

For starters, the drive and desire I felt (and that you probably feel) to get to know and spend time with someone special is completely normal. It's one of the natural things that happens as you mature, like no longer being scared by cooties. Curiosity and interest in the opposite sex electrifies you, and you long to pursue male-female friendships.

What's the source of this desire to date and what awakens our romantic feelings? I believe both are prompted by our God-given need for companionship. As Stuart Briscoe writes in *What It Means to Be Real,* "Scripture makes it very clear that our lives are lived in terms of relationships: with God and with human beings."

God created us with the capacity for companionship, including the capacity for romantic feelings. These feelings are natural and can teach us a lot about ourselves and others. Without them, we could easily get caught up in ourselves and never invest in relationships. We might become terribly selfish and neglect our need to grow in humility and service to others.

So you don't need to feel bad because you want to date someone. It isn't sinful to have romantic feelings. God knows the desires of your heart. Even better, He wants to fulfill those desires when you walk with Him. Look at Psalm 37:4: "Delight yourself in the LORD, and he will give you the desires of your heart." You *did* read that right. God longs to fulfill the desires of your heart.

This verse isn't an assurance that your every wish will come true; just because you desire to date a certain person doesn't mean God will send him or her knocking on your door. But God *does* want to see you contented and fulfilled. And He knows better than you what you need and should want in a mate.

Just think: In this area of your life, as much as in any other, you have the all-knowing, all-wise Creator of everything as your Guide. That's so reassuring and refreshing.

BECAUSE GOD IS LOVE

But it really isn't enough just to say romantic feelings are natural. It's not even enough to say God knows you want to date. Romantic feelings are acceptable because God Himself *is love,* and He created us to experience and reflect this aspect of His personality.

Maybe you're familiar with Genesis 1:27: "God created man in his own image." Our bodies and minds reflect the nature of God, who sees, hears, and *feels.* Because God is love, we can feel love.

More important, however, being created in His image and reborn as Christians means our spirits are modeled after God's Spirit. Because God is love, we can and *must* love.

In 1 John 4:7-8 we're commanded to "love one another, for love comes from God. Everyone who loves has been born of God and knows God. Whoever does not love does not know God, because God is love." Pretty clear, isn't it? The Lord wants us to love. He isn't talking in those verses about romantically loving everyone. But our Father *has* given us the desire and drive not only for brotherly love but also for romantic love. Why?

Because in the Scriptures we learn that romantic love, in a deep and mysterious way, is intended to reflect God's love for the church, Christ's bride for eternity.

In fact, your romantic love toward another person can honor God because it shows Him that you consider His precious creation to be valuable and worthy, just as God does.

God wants us to love, and as part of that love, He wants us to experience romance. He designed it, modeled it, and made it to last!

THE STRENGTH OF LOVE

But what exactly is this great thing called "love"? Dictionaries define it with phrases like "a warm liking or affection," "a tender or passionate affection," "a warm feeling," "a strong liking." To me, those descriptions sound a little weak.

When we look at God's definition, however, we see more clearly why love is something everyone desires and seeks: True love "always protects, always trusts, always hopes, always perseveres. Love never fails" (1 Corinthians 13:7-8).

True love is tough! To really love, you've got to be willing to sacrifice. As Jesus told us in John 15:13, "Greater love has no one than this, that he lay down his life for his friends." That's some serious commitment.

Maybe you feel you can never live up to that kind of true love in a dating relationship. Don't worry; you don't have to be able to love perfectly in order to date. But if you're willing to work at knowing and following God's guidelines, you can learn to love appropriately.

THE PROBLEM

Yes, romantic love is a wonderful part of human life. And if it weren't for sin, we would be able to love purely and to experience romantic relationships perfectly. Unfortunately, sin has corrupted God's perfect design for love and companionship on this earth. Because we're sinful creatures, our love can be sinful and often is.

But Christ died to redeem us from our sinful desires. By His power and strength within us, we can choose to live holy lives full of love and God-honoring romance. As long as we rely on the Holy Spirit to guide us, we don't have to be afraid to pursue romance in dating.

Instead of denying or repressing your romantic feelings, you need to learn to bring them under the Lord's control. All your thoughts on this subject can be in line with God's perspective as you "take captive every thought to make it obedient to Christ" (2 Corinthians 10:5).

God created you with romantic feelings, and now He wants you to give them back to Him so He can help you date and learn to love according to His standards. But godly dating doesn't happen automatically; it takes work. Even though your desire for romance isn't sinful, your response to these deep feelings can cross God's boundary lines. You can date foolishly. You can be drawn into compromising with the world. If you become involved in inappropriate emotional or physical intimacy, you can and will sin against God.

So we have to be careful to guard against any sin, small or great, that would steal our affection from the Lord. By paying attention to the principles you'll see in this book, you can stay within God's boundaries and date to His glory.

LOOKING AHEAD...

So here at this crossroads in your life, it's time to put the signposts back up. We need solid directions for issues such as...
- knowing what a "date" really is.
- figuring out what to do on a real-life date and how to treat the person you're with.
- meeting your responsibilities before, during, and after a date.
- determining when you're ready for dating.
- following God's standards and knowing what will result if you do—or if you don't.
- establishing good boundaries, both emotionally and physically, and learning how to protect them.

These are just a few of the places we're headed in the chapters to come. I trust you're as eager as I am to start the journey.

According to Webster

You Call That a Date?

When I was in high school, I struggled to draw a line between dates and just-friends activities with girls. My junior prom is a perfect example.

When prom season came around that year, I wasn't interested in anyone in particular. Becky sat next to me in English, and we always had fun, so we decided to go to the prom together as "just friends." (I know you recognize that problematic phrase.)

Becky had just broken up with Jeff, her longtime boyfriend. Jeff and I had never gotten along, and when he found out about our prom plans, he took it upon himself to warn me (it was more like a threat) that if I made any moves on Becky, he'd blah, blah, blah. I assured him I had no feelings for his ex-girlfriend. And that was the truth; my intentions were to enjoy the prom and hang with my buddies. Becky was a nice girl, and I enjoyed her friendship, but I didn't want more than that.

Prom night arrived, and I sported the tuxedo I'd rented to match

Becky's sequined gown. The night should have been fun and a great memory. Unfortunately, Becky and I seemed to have different definitions of "just friends." All night she inched closer and closer. I tried to come up with new ways to signal that I just wasn't interested, without having to actually say it. The only thing that saved me was that the night had an end (our curfew).

I thought we both understood that we were just friends. But things are never that simple when guy-girl relationships are involved. Both Becky and I ended up frustrated simply because we were operating with different definitions and intentions. We hadn't made sure that we were on the same wavelength. Of course it didn't help when some of our friends assumed that just because we were prom dates, the next step was a promise ring.

Defining the boundaries of guy-girl relationships can be complicated. What is a date, really? Can you "go out" as friends? How do you deal with buddies who are ready to marry you off to someone you take to the prom?

I believe we'll never get these things straight without a good working definition of a date.

WHAT YOU TOLD ME

In researching for this book, I surveyed about a thousand young adults between the ages of fourteen and twenty-five. Question number one asked them to define what constituted a date.

"I don't really know," a twenty-two-year-old female responded. "It always seems sketchy when it's not clearly defined." She wasn't alone. Around 90 percent of those I surveyed found it hard to define the word *date*.

And those who did define it came up with a whole range of definitions, from the simple "spending time with special attention to a person of the opposite sex" (that's from a fifteen-year-old female) to the more intense "time set apart...with emphasis on a possible future together, and having fun while doing it" (from a male, twenty-five).

One person defined it as "a way of looking for someone you are compatible with...usually romantic, but not always." Okay, but what happens if one person thinks they're on a romantic date and the other doesn't?

Another identified a date as a "time where you and your potential wife/husband go off with a group of friends to get to know each other in a better way." Whoa. That could be kind of weighty. How does marriage enter the picture?

Obviously there are many diverse definitions of dating. Each of these definitions clues us in to different aspects of what a date can be while also pointing to various stages of dating, from the simple to the serious. But there doesn't seem to be a widely accepted standard for what a date really is.

SIMPLER THAN YOU THOUGHT

You may be as shocked as I was to see how dictionaries define *date*. It's totally simple: "a prearranged social engagement" or "an appointment to meet socially." That's it. Nothing more than a social time agreed upon beforehand.

Isn't it nice to see a definition so straightforward, uncomplicated, and broad? It encompasses everything from grabbing coffee to sharing an elaborate candlelit dinner.

It seems to me that the basic definition of *dating* is much less complicated than we've made it. We should be able to tell pretty quickly whether something is a date or not. If it's prearranged and social, it's a date.

MORE RESPONSIBILITY

"Wow," you may be thinking, "so much of what I do is really dating, according to that definition." You're right. I think you'll realize that, once you look at it more realistically, dating may be a bigger part of your day-to-day life than you thought. Even a group of friends getting together after a football game could be a group date. And a prom is definitely date material.

But this broader and simpler understanding of dating brings with it greater responsibility. Since according to this definition many of your activities are dates, you need to clearly communicate your intentions to the person you want to be with. Clarity and honesty are of utmost importance.

Think about how your actions and words will come across to this person. There are obvious things you can do to clearly communicate your intentions. If you think he or she might assume that your invitation to go out for dinner is a bigger deal than you intend, then either clarify what you mean or don't extend the invitation. If you just want to hang out as friends, make it a group activity, because most people think one-on-one time means something more. If, after the first date with someone, you know you don't want a second date, then don't say, "I'll call." But if you say you'll call, then make sure you do.

By operating according to this simpler and broader definition— and accepting the responsibility that goes with it—you'll face less pressure and stress in dating. This should free you to date without overblown expectations and anxiety. You'll be able to sidestep many of the misunderstandings and troubles that can come with dating.

YOUR WORRY-FREE PHILOSOPHY

I'm blown away when I consider the massive amounts of time and energy spent on dating and how stressed people can get about it. For the past decade I've watched young people lose sleep, check out of school, lose touch with their families, and worry themselves sick, all because of dating.

There's no place for worry in a Christian's life. "Do not be anxious about anything," God exhorts us in Philippians 4:6, "but in everything, by prayer and petition, with thanksgiving, present your requests to God."

What is it you're so concerned about when it comes to dating? Is it that you aren't good enough to date someone? That you haven't been asked out? That you don't know whether a certain person likes you or not? Take those concerns to God. The more time you spend in prayer, the more you'll sense God's peace about these issues.

On the other hand, the more stressed you are about dating, the more consumed you become with it. Dating can become a god in your life. If you find yourself thinking more about your date than the Lord, your priorities are out of balance. If you spend hours planning a date, but no time alone with God, are you keeping Him first?

To you, His child, God says, "You shall have no other gods before me" (Exodus 20:3). Don't place your dating life ahead of your Lord.

If you recognize anxiety in your dating life, I suggest you evaluate whether you're acting more self-centered than God-centered. Worrying about dating is essentially focusing on yourself.

And beware. When it comes to dating, Satan would like to keep you anxious and confused. So you need to keep things in perspective. Never let dating become so huge in your life that you lose sight of what's far more important—your relationship with God.

Dating by Whose Rules?

For That Great First Impression—Think Again

When I was sixteen, getting my driver's license meant more than being free to go out with my friends. It also meant I could finally date for real. I could actually pick a girl up and take her somewhere. I didn't have to rely on my brother David to shuttle us around. (Besides, I was getting tired of washing his car as a thank-you.)

My Uncle Harold graciously loaned me his 1963 Chevy Impala until I could buy a car of my own. What a man! He gave me freedom in the form of that Chevy.

A few months after I got my license, I had my first date with Christine, a girl I knew from the ice-cream and sandwich shop where we both worked. She was the first girl to ride in my new mean machine.

The Impala was a stick shift with a 327-cubic-inch engine and a four-speed Muncie (if you know what that is, guys). Christine lived on one of the steeper hills in the area. As you can imagine, the combination of stick shift and steep hill spelled disaster for a new driver.

As I drove her home and prepared to park next to her house, I let the clutch out just a bit too early. The car slammed into the curb and threw us into the air. I looked over at Christine just as her head bounced off the ceiling.

Christine screamed as if the car might go right through her front door. To be honest, I wondered if it might.

It took Christine about five minutes to settle down. Eventually she got up the strength to get out of my car. I'm sure when she recounted the story to her family and friends they all got a great laugh at my expense.

I wasn't laughing. In fact, I remember driving home lamenting that I'd broken what I considered an important rule in dating: Always make a good impression, especially if it's your first.

THE RULES ARE REAL

Whether we like it or not, there are rules for almost everything in life. Board games, schools, even wars have codified systems of what's acceptable and what's not.

Dating is no exception. Much of our culture's dating ritual is based on rules and requirements. For example, worldly dating gives top priority to external impressions and appearances. Two people on a date are expected to please and impress each other in all the outward ways. But is "Thou must impress thy date" one of God's rules? No. God tells us to focus on what's within.

When you date, as with everything else in life, you're following a set of rules and standards—although you may not be conscious of them. Whether deliberately chosen or not, your dating rules will reflect either the world's values, God's values, or a dangerous combination of both.

Let's take a look at some of the most common rules in the dating world and what God has to say about them:

THE WORLD'S DATING RULES:	GOD'S DATING RULES:
Please and impress with outward appearances. Make a good first impression. Image is everything.	*Look at the heart.* "The LORD does not look at the things man looks at. Man looks at the outward appearance, but the LORD looks at the heart" (1 Samuel 16:7).
Live for the moment. Just do it. Now is the time.	*Live for God's will.* The Christian "does not live the rest of his earthly life for evil human desires, but rather for the will of God" (1 Peter 4:2). The Lord teaches us to be patient and to delay gratification.
Look out for Number One. What have you done for me lately? What can I get out of this?	*Look out for others.* "Do nothing out of selfish ambition or vain conceit, but in humility consider others better than yourselves" (Philippians 2:3). Always seek first to serve and give to others.
Play games. Flirt. Play hard to get. Play the field.	*Be real and honest.* "Therefore each of you must put off falsehood and speak truthfully to his neighbor, for we are all members of one body" (Ephesians 4:25).
Follow your heart and your feelings. If it feels right, do it. Anything's okay if you're in love.	*Follow Him.* "My son, do not forget my teaching, but keep my commands in your heart, for they will prolong your life many years and bring you prosperity" (Proverbs 3:1-2).

This isn't an exhaustive list of the world's dating rules, but it covers some of the more prevalent lies—especially those last two, playing games and following your heart. In fact, let's take a closer look at those two false commandments.

PLAYING GAMES: FLIRTING WITH DISASTER

A local middle school printed a Valentine's Day newspaper. The pages were full of the world's lie that playing games is the best way to interact with the opposite sex. In a section entitled "Dear Destiny," one student wrote:

> Dear Destiny,
>   I like this guy so much. He flirts with me a lot. But I don't want to ask him out and ruin our friendship. What should I do?

"Destiny" responded with this advice:

> Flirt with him back. Flirting is the ultimate way to get someone to like you. If you ask him out, it probably won't ruin the friendship. He's probably thinking the same thing you are.

Flirting is not honest communication; it's manipulation. Don't follow Destiny's bad advice and try to charm a person into liking you. You end up playing mind games. That kind of relationship is doomed to end quickly because it's not based on truth.

In a book called *A Fine Romance*, psychologist Judith Sills noted that dating involves so much game playing "that you sometimes feel the last person to know the real you would be someone you are dating." However, this "ritualized behavior" has a purpose, the author decided: "It helps you take the risk of becoming involved in the first place. It gives you a safe role to assume."

I don't think it should be this way. Instead of flirting, win people with who you truly are. The most attractive person is someone who's real, someone who doesn't feel the need to impress with flirting or other games.

God never wants you to present yourself as anything but who you are. He doesn't want you playing games to start a relationship. If you feel the need to impress someone by being something you're not, the relationship probably isn't worth pursuing.

FOLLOWING YOUR FEELINGS: IT'S EVERYWHERE

The second lie—the one about following your heart and your feelings—is perhaps the most prevalent of the world's lies today. The message is prominent in music, television, books, and movies.

In *The Phantom Menace,* a supposedly wise Jedi knight advises Anakin Skywalker, "Don't think. Feel." The young boy goes on to win the race, and the audience is left to conclude that he succeeded because he let his emotions control his mind. Yeah, right!

Or take the chapel scene in *The Mask of Zorro.* Zorro and the heroine had previously met one another, and there was an immediate connection and attraction between the two. Later, Zorro hides from trouble by going into a confessional booth in the chapel. The young heroine happens to be on the other side, ready to confess her sins. Thinking he's the priest, she tells Zorro that she's had impure thoughts about a man. (Who do you suppose that could be?) Obviously flattered, Zorro responds, "Senorita, the only sin would be to deny what is in your heart." Where's my barf bag?

You should never justify sin, as Zorro did, because of your feelings. God tells us to obey. He never says, "Obey, unless your heart carries you away." Following your heart means obeying your feelings instead of obeying God. And though feelings often seem impossible to overcome, they aren't.

Only living by God's standards will honor Him and help us avoid sin. So be on guard, and don't mess with the world or try combining its infectious standards with God's truth.

SOME RULES DON'T WORK

So how exactly can you follow God's ways when it comes to dating?

Many Christians have tried to develop the perfect formula for godly dating. One of my mentors, Doug Haag, called this approach "dating by the numbers," like the paint-by-the-numbers books that tell you which color to fill in where. Many Christians try to order their dating lives around a series of dogmatic codes.

When I lived in California, the administration at a Christian school near my home ruled that no boy and girl could sit next to each other without the width of a Bible between them. (Were they talking about a pocket testament or an expanded study edition?) No doubt the administrators believed their rule would prevent lust or at least keep couples from touching. But it didn't. The rule failed to encourage obedience to God's standard of purity, and in fact some guys and girls sat closer than they normally might have just because the rule seemed so ridiculous.

This same focus on perfect formulas makes some Christians think that not dating will keep them from sin. They set up rules such as "Don't ever be alone," "Only group date," and "Just write letters."

These Christians often fall into the trap of legalism, assuming that living by a set of rules equals a godly life. They're drawn to legalism because they think rules and codes simplify life. They have good intentions, but their formulaic approach falls short.

Paul talks about this in Colossians 2:20-23, where he lists the rules, "Do not handle! Do not taste! Do not touch!" Then he writes, "These are all destined to perish with use, because they are based on human commands and teachings. Such regulations indeed have an appearance of wisdom, with their self-imposed worship, their false humility and their harsh treatment of the body, but they lack any value in restraining sensual indulgence." Paul didn't even concede that legalistic rules were helpful to some degree. Look again at his last words about them: "*They lack any value* in restraining sensual indulgence."

Philip Yancey emphasizes this point in his book *What's So Amazing About Grace?* Yancey writes, "Legalism fails miserably at the one thing it is supposed to do: encourage obedience.... A system of strict laws actually puts new ideas of lawbreaking in a person's mind."

When it comes to godly dating, a strict formula simply doesn't exist. Of course there are certain nonnegotiables that a Christian must follow, such as focusing first on God and maintaining purity. But having rules doesn't prevent you from sinning. Only a heart inclined to God can.

So don't base your dating life on "human commands and teachings," even if they come from well-meaning Christians. I encourage you: Don't listen to anyone's rules or formulas without checking them against the Word of God. For dating success, we need to challenge the world's lies with God's Word, not with any legalistic formula.

GOD'S GRACE IS YOUR FREEDOM

The opposite of legalism is grace. Grace is freedom. Grace is risky business, however; it's been called "scandalous" and "dangerous."

Some Christians abuse God's grace by dating recklessly and using their freedom to justify a loose life. It ends up making a mess of relationships and lives. Other Christians observe this and come up with legalistic rules, including the rule to abstain from dating entirely. But God didn't design our freedom to work this way.

Freedom in Christ doesn't mean living by a list, but neither does it mean doing whatever you please. Freedom in Christ means developing personal convictions about certain areas, for instance, dating according to the Word of God. You don't have to focus on what others are doing or saying. As Chuck Swindoll writes (in the Bible study guide to his book *The Grace Awakening*), "With our freedom in Christ...we are free to make good, objective choices. We are able to think independently without the tyranny of needing to compare ourselves with others."

You are accountable to God. He's given you the ability to make good decisions about dating. He will help you find the right balance between the extremes of dating any way you please and ditching dating altogether. He will help you live in His grace.

YOUR CHALLENGE

In this chapter you've seen two pitfalls of dating by the rules. You can play by the world's rules of dating and fall into irresponsibility and the abuse of grace. Or you can play the legalistic Christian game, focusing on rules to solve what is really a matter of the heart.

As an alternative to these extremes, I want to issue you this threefold challenge:

1. *Obey God*—because *His* standards set us free. "I run in the path of your commands, for you have set my heart free!... Your statutes are wonderful; therefore I obey them" (Psalm 119:32,129).

2. *Live in grace, not legalism.* "It is for freedom that Christ has set us free. Stand firm, then, and do not let yourselves be burdened again by a yoke of slavery" (Galatians 5:1).

3. *Please God, not people.* "If I were still trying to please men, I would not be a servant of Christ" (Galatians 1:10).

Remember, it's God's standards that count, not someone else's— even if you know they're laughing at your driving.

Choosing Your Date

First Things First

It had been a long day at work, and I finally started relaxing as I listened to phone messages on my answering machine at home. My ears perked up as a strange female voice came over the recorder.

"Jeramy Clark, I've got something for you. Call me back when you can, at 555-4376." Click.

She left no name. I racked my brain trying to figure out who it could be. Someone from work? No, I knew everyone there well enough to recognize their voices. A long-lost friend from high school? That seemed doubtful, because she probably would have mentioned it. It wasn't a wrong number, because this woman said my name. The message couldn't have been from a telemarketer either, because they never ask you to call them back. (They just play that little game to catch you the moment dinner's on the table.)

I was totally intrigued.

After a bit of pondering, I called the number. The same female voice greeted me on the other end. We quickly discovered that she had been trying to reach a different Jeramy Clark. How weird is that?

We laughed for a few minutes about the misunderstanding, but didn't hang up right away. In fact, we had an interesting conversation. Kayla and I discovered quickly that we shared a faith in Christ. She was currently enrolled at a Christian college near my house. The more we talked, the more we seemed to connect.

At some point in the conversation, we decided we had to meet. Surely the sheer coincidence of it all warranted that, I reasoned. It seemed kind of funny to me—a blind date set up by an answering machine.

A few days later I picked up Kayla in front of her college dorm. We had chosen to grab coffee together and chat—a no-pressure, low-romance situation in my mind.

But I soon realized Kayla and I had never talked about age. She sounded a lot older on the phone. Yes, she was in college, but she was only a freshman—barely older than the students I served at the church. I knew I shouldn't go out with Kayla again, but I also didn't want to hurt her feelings. The situation was delicate, yet I needed to establish that this wouldn't be an ongoing dating relationship.

That wasn't an easy situation to handle. It sure would have been simpler if I'd never responded to her call.

That incident made me rethink how and why I choose dates. I didn't know anything about Kayla—what kind of family she came from, what types of people she befriended, or even how closely she walked with Christ. I had simply been intrigued by a random coincidence.

Looking back, I regret my decision to pursue a date with her. Where was the wisdom in it? All kinds of things could have happened. She could've been the type of person to spread rumors and slander my character. And I could have left her disappointed or brokenhearted after initiating a date with apparent interest and then immediately backing off.

Fortunately, neither of those things happened. The Lord actually used the situation to remind me that He has a standard for how and why I should choose dates.

How Do You Choose a Date?

How do *you* choose a date? Is your decision based on first impressions—looks, voice, or whatever? Is it because you're attracted to a person's reputation or how well he or she has mastered a certain sport or skill? While being drawn to a person for these reasons isn't wrong, basing a dating relationship on them can be. God wants you to get beyond the surface.

Maybe the other person's qualities have little to do with your choice. You just want to date so badly that you choose dates at random. Whoever asks or consents is okay. You just want "someone." Dating purely because you "really want a relationship" is basically looking for love or fulfillment outside of the Lord. Trust me, you're not going to find it there.

The Ultimate Standard

Before you can even think about choosing a date, I believe you must get the following issues right in your relationship with God.

Jesus tells us, "'Love the Lord your God with all your heart and with all your soul and with all your mind.' This is the first and greatest commandment. And the second is like it: 'Love your neighbor as yourself.' All the Law and the Prophets hang on these two commandments" (Matthew 22:37-40).

God's desire is that you love Him first and most, with all your heart, soul, and mind. In loving Him this way, you'll learn to follow the second commandment to "love your neighbor as yourself." Jesus says this second commandment is like the first. He puts loving others in the same league with loving God. The key to successful relationships with others is a right relationship with God.

Jesus also calls us to love people as He Himself would. In fact, He commands us, "As I have loved you, so you must love one another" (John 13:34).

Isn't it great to know that God's standard boils down to two commandments—to love Him completely and to love others as He does? These principles are not too complicated or confusing, and by following them you can have peace and joy in every area of your life. But, if you're anything like me, you probably want to know more about how to realistically obey these commands day by day.

HOW TO SHOW HIM YOU LOVE HIM

We know God loves us because His Word tells us so. Remember singing as a child, "Jesus loves me; this I know, for the Bible tells me so"? (Doesn't that bring back great memories of graham crackers and apple juice?)

So you know God loves you. But how does He know if you love Him—and with all your heart, soul, and mind as He commands? I doubt you've written a Bible-length love letter to God lately.

The Lord knows that you love Him when you do what He says. In John 14:15, Jesus says, "If you love me, you will obey what I command."

Obedience is a crucial element of your love for God. When you obey, you show the Lord that you take His commands seriously and that you consider His ways better than your own. Your obedience displays humility, for by obeying God you acknowledge that He is God and you are not.

Of course, to respond obediently you need to know *what* to obey. And that's what we discover in God's Word. "How can a young man keep his way pure? By living according to your word.... I have hidden your word in my heart that I might not sin against you" (Psalm 119:9,11).

You love God by learning what His Word commands you to do and then doing it! So bury yourself in His Word. Know it inside and out, and put it into practice. You'll see your life change, and your love for God will grow.

And what about loving others? How do you live according to that commandment?

As I've mentioned, the best way to love others is to love God first. Once you reach up to Him, you'll be filled by Him and enabled to reach out to others.

God knows you love Him when you follow His example. Jesus said, "Greater love has no one than this, that he lay down his life for his friends" (John 15:13). That's exactly what Jesus did for you and me, His friends. The Lord sacrificed all for you; doesn't He deserve *your* all as well?

BACK TO DATING

Now let's focus again on dating. The commandment to love others must be applied to your dating life. Consider every conversation and phone call an opportunity to practice unselfishness. If you're going to love your neighbor as yourself, think about the time you spend together as a chance to practice loving as God does, purely and sacrificially.

For everything you do as you date, ask yourself the basic question, *Would I want someone doing this to me?*

- Would I want someone flirting with me constantly, but never pursuing anything further?
- Would I want someone playing "hard to get" or acting as if he or she could care less whether I called?
- Would I want someone pressuring me into an impure physical relationship or pushing my boundary lines?
- Would I want someone to break my heart?

Remember, God's ultimate standard comes down to this: Love God and love others. If you truly love God first, you'll lay down your life and obey Him. When you've done that, you'll be able to love others as He loves them. You'll treat them as you want to be treated.

DOES THIS MEAN I CAN'T DATE NON-CHRISTIANS?

Even if you truly want to love God obediently and to love others as yourself, a certain dating issue may make your obedience more difficult. I'm talking about dating nonbelievers.

Listen to some biblical guidelines on this, as translated by Eugene Peterson in *The Message:*

> Don't become partners with those who reject
> God. How can you make a partnership out of right
> and wrong? That's not partnership; that's war. Is light
> best friends with dark? Does Christ go strolling

with the Devil? Do trust and mistrust hold hands?
(2 Corinthians 6:14)

As a Christian, you are the "right," the "light," and the "trust" in that passage. And who do you think is represented by the "wrong," the "dark," and the "mistrust"? You've got it: non-Christians. Or as this passage calls them, "those who reject God."

God doesn't want us to be partners with non-Christians. God doesn't want us to be best friends with them, or to stroll with them, or to hold their hands. (Can you see how this could have something to do with dating?)

In my surveys of students, I asked them whether they would date non-Christians. Although the question was of the "circle Y or N" variety, many chose to write in the margin such comments as these: "Yes, unfortunately," and "Yes, against my better judgment," and "Yes, but I would try and change him [or her]."

The response of one sixteen-year-old girl broke my heart. She circled N, then jotted down these words: "I got lied to. The person I was dating said [he was] and pretended to be a Christian. I didn't realize 'til it was too late, and it took me a year and three months to be strong enough to leave, 'cause I fell in love." Experience taught this young woman that dating and falling in love with a non-Christian is painful.

That kind of relationship is not a partnership; it's war, just as 2 Corinthians 6 promises. And in any war, you suffer casualties.

ANCIENT WARNINGS

In the Bible we see how this same war was raging long ago. God warned the Israelites not to marry those who didn't share their faith.

Tragically, the Old Testament records how many people came to ruin because they chose to ignore this instruction.

We also read how King Solomon, the wisest man who ever lived, fell into sin because of "partnerships" with the wrong women. At the end of his life, Solomon cried out that all these relationships intended for pleasure were "meaningless," like a "chasing after the wind" (Ecclesiastes 1:2,17).

Don't be fooled into thinking that as long as you don't marry the person, a dating relationship with a non-Christian is okay. You don't have to marry someone to compromise the Lord's ultimate standard. Scripture records that Solomon had relationships with quite a number of women, most of whom were unbelieving women he never married. Solomon compromised both inside and outside of marriage.

As he became more and more attached to his wives and girlfriends, Solomon turned from the true God and began to worship these women's idols. God then punished him by splitting Solomon's kingdom. What a sad end to the story of a man whom God had blessed so richly.

TOO HARSH?

So I have to take a pretty hard line on this issue of dating non-Christians. The Word of God is clear and straightforward on this topic. Christians are commanded, "Do not be yoked together with unbelievers" (2 Corinthians 6:14).

I believe it's *never* right for a Christian to pursue or carry on a dating relationship with a non-Christian. You may think that's harsh, especially in light of the simple definition of dating we discussed earlier. I'm not saying you shouldn't associate with non-Christians, and I'm not setting down a legalistic rule that it's always wrong to be in a prearranged social situation involving non-Christians of the opposite sex. But you do need to carefully consider the amount and type of time you spend with them.

If you're trying to change or save non-Christians, dating is not the way to do it. I don't believe God has given us the option of "missionary dating." If anything, you're more likely to be converted to the world's way of looking at things. Just how seriously do you think an unbeliever will take your faith if one minute you're messing around physically, and the next you're inviting him or her to church? Think about it—seriously.

The Bible says Christians are a people "belonging to," or set apart for, God (1 Peter 2:9). Your life is *different!* It's true: You can't live just like everyone else. You're called to something higher, something better.

You're called to please God. But if you're in a relationship with an unbeliever, who is your date trying to please? Non-Christians can't share your desire to honor and obey God first. Most likely, they'll be looking out only for themselves.

Consider how being partners with non-Christians—"unequally yoked"—breaks both of the greatest commandments Jesus taught us.

First, dating non-Christians tells God that your own desires are more important than your love for Him. It communicates that His commands aren't worth your obedience and reverence. Are you ready to tell God that?

Dating non-Christians also breaks the second commandment to "love your neighbor as yourself." Dating a non-Christian can actually push that person farther away from Christ, which is the most unloving thing you could do. Your relationship can distract the person away from Jesus or, worse, tarnish the Lord's image in that person's mind. Are you willing to take on that responsibility?

In a later chapter we'll see just how destructive it can be to compromise who you are for what you want. Meanwhile, as a Christian you need to commit now—for all time—that you'll stay "equally yoked" by following God's ultimate standard.

If you love God with your whole life, you'll be "yoked" with Him. That's your starting point. Then you can move on to loving others, always balanced by the love and truth of God. His ultimate standard—to love Him and love others—is the key to the good life in dating relationships and everything else.

Relationship Interviews

GETTING PERSONAL

I started my first job at age eight. I can't remember whether I interviewed for the position, but if I did, the meeting probably went something like this: "You ride a bike? Good. Here's the route. Do it!"

Yes, I began my illustrious career as a paperboy. I'd rise before dawn, fold the *Gazette,* and ride off into the sunrise. Usually I'd end my morning run with an apple fritter and milk at the doughnut shop down the street. I felt so grown up.

The older I got, the more serious my jobs became. By the time I graduated from high school, I had almost ten years of work experience. I knew not only how to work, but also how to interview.

Shortly after high-school graduation, I spotted an ad in the newspaper: "Sell Sports Equipment. Make $12.50/hr.!" I thought about it for a minute, then jotted down the number.

Why not? I enjoyed sales because of the contact with people, and sports equipment could be fun. And the $12.50 per hour really caught my attention. Minimum wage at that time was hanging around four bucks. I could triple that with this sales job.

I called the number and spoke to a representative. I didn't catch the name of the company, but I was asked to come down for a personal interview. Drawn by the possibilities, I donned my one suit, groomed myself to a T, and headed off. I didn't realize what an adventure I had begun.

The interview wasn't as personal as I'd expected. About twenty other people sat around waiting for their names to be called. My time eventually came, and I answered a few questions.

Minutes later a representative announced that the following people had passed the first screening. He called my name, and I admit I felt pretty excited. He gathered us together, telling us we had the "style" and "finesse" they wanted. My anticipation increased.

He instructed us to come back in one hour, after which our first round of training would begin. It struck me as somewhat odd that I'd start training so soon for a job I knew nothing about, but an hour later I was back.

The training session opened with a few introductions and the like. Then, out of nowhere, our training leader shifted into infomercial mode. He held out a coin and asked, "If I could cut through this quarter, would you be impressed?"

The group replied somewhat tentatively, "Yeah, okay." Then he pulled out a set of knives and scissors. He took the scissors and ripped through that quarter like it was paper.

I was wondering when he would show us the sports equipment, but it didn't take long before he had mesmerized everyone in the room with his fast-talking, quarter-cutting energy. With one of the knives, he sliced through metal, thick rope, and various other uncuttable objects. Then to show us the blade hadn't dulled, he took a tomato to the chopping block and sliced it with graceful ease.

He revealed to us that his company had invented the "knife set of the future." As he praised these instruments of culinary wonder that would revolutionize the world, he held our attention by asking us questions and bouncing beads off the table toward anyone who answered correctly. He told us we'd win prizes for the number of beads we collected.

By now I had completely forgotten about sports equipment. This guy convinced me I had to be part of the brightest light on the horizon: KNIVES. When he asked each of us for twenty dollars to ensure our support, I handed over the money without much thought.

During a break in the "training," I called my parents, eager to share with them my good news.

My father seemed less than thrilled. "No way, Jer. This is the dumbest thing I've ever heard. Who are these clowns?"

His disbelief didn't faze me. "Dad," I started, "they said my parents might not understand. I'm gonna make millions. I just gave them a twenty for training supplies, so—"

"What?" he bellowed into the phone. "I thought you were interviewing to *make* money, Jeramy, not give it away! Son, I'm telling you—get out while you can."

We hung up. With Dad's words ringing in my head, I headed back into that training room filled with giddy, knife-loving people. I had to stop and think. Was selling knives what I really wanted? Was I ready to go door-to-door asking people if I could cut through quarters for them? Why had I given this guy twenty bucks?

I started getting angry. Their ad talked about sports equipment; they said I'd make money; they told me I had style and finesse. But it was all a show. I'd been tricked! They just wanted to suck me into the world of knives. The fiends!

During the next break, I asked the trainer for my money back. I simply didn't want the position, I told him. After trying a few of his magical infomercial moves on me, he agreed to refund my twenty, but asked me to leave quietly so as not to spoil the others' fun.

That experience taught me a lot. I'd always heard that while being interviewed, you interview the company as well. If I'd just remembered that advice, I could have seen through their dazzle-me tactics before spending a whole day listening to phony promises of happiness and fulfillment.

I've since heard that the company does extremely well and that their knives really are of superior quality. That didn't really matter though. I didn't want to join forces with the kind of company I saw on display during that interview. It just wasn't a match. Thanks to my dad's sound advice, I didn't buy into the knife-selling dream.

EXPLORING THE OPTION

During a job interview, both you and the company explore the possibility of uniting forces. If you decide to work for them, you join their team. You have to believe in the company, their product, and their vision for the future.

Along the same lines, have you ever thought of dates as "relationship interviews"? Just as if you'd applied for a job, you and your date interview one another, trying to figure out if you're a match. If the interview goes well, there may be more.

Not only your first date with someone, but every future date with that person can serve as a relationship interview. Eventually you may even decide to join forces and become a couple. Or, as I discovered in the knife saga, sometimes you realize that you just don't click.

Hopefully, dating won't be as formal or frightening as interviewing for a job often is. You don't have to impress anyone; just be yourself! Dating should be an easygoing yet purposeful time to get to know another person.

The more you interview someone, the more you learn about him or her. The process never stops. With each relationship interview you have the opportunity to dig deeper and discover more about who that person is.

AVOID THE FRUSTRATION

Picture yourself going out with someone a few times, maybe even becoming boyfriend-girlfriend. You take in a few movies and a little Friday night bowling and Starbucks now and then.

Then one day you figure out you've never had a real conversation with that person. You didn't know that he or she is a communist! Okay, maybe it's not that bad, but you do discover that you have vastly different goals, dreams, and values. You're together, but there's not much to seriously talk about.

This can be pretty frustrating if you've been dating for a while. You've invested time in someone who's nowhere near to being right for you, and now you regret it.

You can avoid such situations by thinking "interview." But don't think of it as "I'm trying to figure out if you're good enough for me." That kind of arrogant attitude will turn people away for sure. Think of a relationship interview as a time to mutually determine whether you want to develop a deeper friendship. Then you'll be better equipped to discern whether someone is a match for you.

PURPOSE AND PLANNING

Looking at dating as an interview process can help you plan and approach each date with purpose. Every interview has a purpose; relationship interviews are no different. Before going out, you have to know what your purpose is. Then you can plan accordingly.

As we saw earlier, the definition of a date is simple. It's just a "pre-arranged social engagement." So keep your dates lighthearted! You don't have to determine on the first date whether you'll marry the person.

You do, however, want to figure out soon if this person is someone you want to spend more time with. That's the fundamental purpose of a date. The aim of a relationship interview is to determine whether you want to further develop the relationship.

Plan according to that purpose. Don't focus on surface issues, such as whether someone eats soup with a spoon or slurps it out of the bowl (I prefer bowl-slurpers). Plan to ask questions about things that are truly important to you.

Just as in a job interview, you must resolve to be yourself in a relationship interview. Don't try to put on some act to win over your interviewer. Playing games destroys true relationship potential. Your date can't really get to know you if you're busy acting like someone you think he or she would like. Likewise, if you're concerned only with how you're acting, you won't be able to interview your date.

So determine ahead of time to be yourself. Resolve not to say you like or dislike something just because the other person does. Plan to speak honestly about yourself and not to exaggerate. Just be you.

Finally, plan to honor the Lord in all your relationship interviews. That includes praying on your own about and for every date. It also includes setting good boundaries beforehand, a topic we'll explore in more detail later in the book.

To sum up:

1. Keep your dates lighthearted.

2. Be yourself.

3. Honor God.

If you do these three things, your relationship interviews will be successful, and you can actually focus on getting to know the other person.

Now let's get into more specifics: the who, what, when, where, why, and how of relationship interviewing.

WHO

Students I minister to sometimes ask me who they should date, assuming I could set them up with Mr. or Ms. Right (as if being in ministry makes me Cupid).

I can't tell anyone exactly who to date, but I can recommend that you date certain types of people.

For starters, let me repeat that Christians are to date Christians only. Never forget what God says in 2 Corinthians 6:14.

But which Christians should you consider? Here's a helpful approach: Think of dating as a race. You're running on your own, then one day you notice someone running next to you at the *same pace* and in the *same direction*. You can run together without hindrance because your course is the same.

That's the kind of person you want to consider as a dating partner. Look for someone who runs at the same pace you do. If you're a growing Christian, look for others who are growing like you. If you're a mature believer, run with another mature Christian who will keep up and even push you to run better.

As for direction, find out if someone's goals and dreams match yours. If his or her primary interest is sports, and you hate anything physical, you may have a hard time connecting. If he or she loves raising farm animals while your dream is to sell high-profile stocks on Wall Street, tensions may arise.

Another great guideline is to check out the person's other relationships. As you do, here are two essential principles to consider:

- "He who walks with the wise grows wise, but a companion of fools suffers harm" (Proverbs 13:20). Does this person hang out with fools? Or are his or her friends respectable and trustworthy?
- "Honor your father and your mother" (Deuteronomy 5:16). The Word of God commands us to respect our parents. Does this person treat his family with dignity and honor? If not, do you think he'll treat you any better after a while?

If you pursue only Christian dates, and if you evaluate your compatibility with that person and observe his or her other relationships, you'll be well on your way to successful relationship interviews.

WHAT

What should you talk about once you're on a date? Let me suggest three basic guidelines:

- Be real. This idea is worth repeating because being yourself is so critically important. You are the best asset you have in a relationship interview.
- Be aware. What you talk about will affect expectations. If you

bring up kissing, what's your date supposed to think? If you mention marriage, your date might easily assume things are more serious than they are.

- Be guarded. Maintain honesty, but don't feel you have to reveal everything about yourself at once. The Word of God tells us, "Guard your heart, for it is the wellspring of life" (Proverbs 4:23).

WHEN

Right off I can think of two big "when" questions. The first is the age issue. What's the right age to begin dating? Let's save that one for a later chapter and look now at the second "when" question.

Since most dates happen at night—dinner, a movie, a dance, etc.—a big issue is how late to stay out. You probably have curfews most of the time, so let me go on record as saying curfews are wonderful. Yes, you read that right.

If you have a curfew, stick to it! Obey your parents on this issue as well as others. Don't simply assume you can "just call" if you're late. Be on time. Doing so will save you from many temptations, as well as from the wrath of upset parents.

When my wife, Jerusha, and I started dating, we were old enough to decide for ourselves when to end our dates. Though we had no one enforcing it, we set a curfew for ourselves. We both agreed that things get more intense the later the hour. If you think about it, I know you'll recognize what I'm talking about. Night covers up and hides many things. We chose to avoid any temptation that could come with late hours, and it worked.

If you're old enough not to have a curfew, or if your parents have never set one, do it for yourself. Do it for your own good. Maintaining purity will be much easier if you set wise limits on how late you stay out.

WHERE

Your location will definitely affect how much fun you'll have and how well you'll get to know the other person. So make sure you plan ahead of time where you're going. Here are some general principles to keep in mind:

- Always opt for a public place. Dates are safer if other people are around. Jerusha and I hung out at Starbucks, where we had some great conversations. (An added bonus: It was inexpensive!)
- Choose places where the environment encourages conversation. Movies are fun, but how well do you get to know someone with both your faces staring at a flick? Jerusha and I liked to walk around her neighborhood on our dates. We could really talk and enjoy the outdoors at the same time.
- Pick a place where you'll feel comfortable. This is much easier if both of you know exactly where you'll be going. Surprises are fine only after trust is earned. Meanwhile, if you find yourself uncomfortable about where you are or where you're going, never be afraid to speak up.

WHY

We've discussed many reasons to go on dates: You can have fun, learn more about each other, and build a relationship. But remember that as Christians our main goal in dating, as in everything else, is not to please ourselves but to please God. If you're dating merely for entertainment value, is it really worthwhile?

Instead of simply looking for fun, seek out opportunities to encourage each other. I'm not talking just about compliments. Keep looking for ways to spur your date on in his or her walk with Christ, as well as in personal goals. Try to uplift your date spiritually.

HOW

You've probably noticed that I've spoken quite a bit about deciding things ahead of time. I've encouraged you to make "predecisions."

Predecisions are just that—choices made ahead of time. You will date most successfully if you decide how you'll conduct yourself before any relationship interview.

Making a predecision prevents you from walking blindly into dangerous situations. Take, for instance, the issue of where. If you know for certain you'll be eating dinner at Claim Jumper and playing a round of miniature golf, you won't have to worry about the two of you ending up alone in an empty house.

Making a predecision also helps you to wisely evaluate each dating opportunity. If you want to focus on getting to know each other, but the person asks you to go to the movies on a first date, you'll be better able to suggest an alternative or just say no.

Making predecisions is easiest when you remember that you are a limited edition, a specialty creation of the Lord God. Don't compromise who you are for the temporary fun of a date. Commit yourself now to making predecisions about your dating life, so you don't get trapped in something that could turn out a lot worse than watching a guy cut through quarters.

Quality Control

SOMEDAY MY PRINCE (OR PRINCESS) WILL COME

Shortly before my nineteenth birthday, I realized my dating life had spun out of control. Actually, my entire life had spiraled downward. I had fallen away from the Lord and found myself hanging with the wrong crowd. I had swallowed the lure of the party scene.

But the partying never satisfied me. I'd accepted Christ early in life and had tasted and seen that the Lord is good. I recognized that the things I was doing were sinful and displeasing to God. I couldn't enjoy that kind of godless lifestyle because I knew the Lord wanted something better for me.

No one needed to quote a chapter or verse to me. The Holy Spirit Himself convicted me each time I pursued the things of the world rather than the things of Christ. I recall lying in bed at night, feeling torn and so far from the Lord.

I was still attending church, because that's what my parents required of me as long as I lived in their home. (I'm grateful for that now.) I never kicked and screamed to get out of it, though I kind of tuned out on Sundays. Except one particular Sunday...

I'll never forget that day when youth pastor Ted Montoya approached me at church with an offer straight from the Lord. "Jeramy," he said, "God has really laid you on my heart. Would you consider working with the high-school ministry?"

I felt like doing backflips up and down the aisle. Ted had thrown me a life preserver with God's fingerprints all over it. Though I had strayed, the Lord faithfully provided a way back.

The next day Ted and I ate lunch at Taco Bell (in the days before the Chihuahua), and we talked through my spiritual issues. I knew the time had come to either devote my life to Christ entirely or check out for good. Either Jesus was the Son of God, or He wasn't. If He was, He deserved my life. He deserved my whole life—who I spent time with, what my future would look like, and even who I would date.

A CHANGED LIFE

Ted's invitation changed my life. I quickly became serious about my faith. I realized that to be an example to students, I needed to live above reproach. I needed to break away from the patterns of ungodliness I had set.

It wasn't easy to cut off my harmful friendships. My old friends didn't really understand, but then how could I expect them to?

The relationship patterns I'd set with girls were especially hard to break. I'd played lots of games while playing the field. But after recommitting my life to Jesus, all my rebellious ways needed to stop—pronto. God was now in control of my dating life, and I needed to wait on Him for direction.

For two years I didn't date at all. Nothing, nada, el zippo. It's not that I made a set-in-stone vow to abstain from dating. But I'd made the commitment to focus on the Lord, and it just so happened that for a while this meant no dating. It was during this time that the Lord cleansed me from a lot of my patterns of dating folly.

I spent time in God's Word, wrestling with His truth, and the Lord began rebuilding my character. He especially used my parents in this; their example gave me something to strive for.

God also used mentors and friends to teach me. I met weekly with Ted, who mentored me personally and spiritually. He taught me about youth ministry and about becoming a man of purpose and vision.

My senior pastor, Dr. Phil Howard, included me in a discipleship class where we studied 1 Timothy. That's where I learned to pray. Dr. Howard always said the only way to learn to pray was to pray with men who knew how. I've got to tell you, Dr. Howard knows how!

Eventually I enrolled in the Master's College. My faith had grown significantly, and I wanted to pursue full-time ministry.

To my delight, many godly young women attended Master's. I enjoyed casual dating by going to the school's spring fling and other such events. It was refreshing to be around women of excellence and to have the option of dating them. These were the kind of women I wanted to attract. In my earlier days, the kinds of girls I attracted were trouble. Now that I was walking with the Lord, I wanted women to be drawn to the man Christ was fashioning in me.

I knew I still had a lot of work ahead of me. My character continued to grow through classes taught by some of the godliest men I've ever known. I also developed close friendships with other students who were men of character and who nourished my own character. Through it all, I consistently spent time with the Great Teacher Himself.

I didn't suddenly become perfect or anything. I still made mistakes. But all the time I'd spent letting God build my character really changed me. Now I could date to His glory, something I knew nothing about earlier.

BEAUTY AND THE BARBARIAN

Think about your own life for a moment. Is your lifestyle going to attract men or women of character? The bottom line is this: If you want to date quality individuals, you've got to be one yourself.

Consider this story:

Once upon a time, a young princess wandered through the woods. A nasty and barbarous man spotted the lovely princess and approached her. He offered her the "pleasure" of becoming his bride and living with him in the shack he called home.

After a quick look at this barbarian and his residence, the princess flatly refused. She told him she would never marry a man who couldn't respect himself or his home. She wanted someone honorable like her father, the king. Then off she went to the beautiful castle.

The barbarian was crushed.

In the following days, he couldn't get the pure and noble princess out of his mind. Finally he vowed to win her, no matter what. He decided the only way to do this was to become a noble man himself.

He observed the king from afar, watching his actions and listening to his speech. He noticed and admired the king's integrity and dignity. The king's character captivated the barbarian. He wanted to be just like him. He still longed to marry the princess, but now his desire to become as noble as the king exceeded even his love for the princess.

Slowly but surely, as the barbarian modeled his behavior after the king, his appearance and manner were refined. He also worked long and hard to transform his home into a beautiful estate surrounded by well-tended gardens.

Finally he felt ready to approach the princess once more. This time the princess was so impressed that she promised to consider his request to become his bride. Eventually the two were wed, and (you guessed it) they lived happily every after.

I'm sure you get the point. The barbarian needed to work on himself before he could attract the princess. Before she would consider marrying him, he needed to develop his character; he needed to be more like the king.

But the barbarian didn't change himself merely "to get the girl." He changed because he admired the king's character and wanted to be like him. Even if the princess rejected him a second time, the barbarian had permanently changed his life for the better. His improved quality of life made all the character work worthwhile.

A SPIRITUAL INVENTORY

As a Christian, your character is shaped by your knowledge and love of our King Jesus Christ. Therefore, building your spiritual character should be your first priority, ahead of developing other relationships.

Like the barbarian, you may want to rush into a relationship with a beautiful princess or a handsome prince. But remember that your identity is based on who you are in Christ, not on who you date. As you get to know the Lord, you'll find security and contentment in Him. As you learn to be okay with God alone, your character will become more and more like His.

You cannot build godly character without knowing God. As Jerry Bridges puts it in *The Practice of Godliness,* "So often we try to develop Christian character without taking time to develop God-centered devotion. We try to please God without taking time to walk with Him and develop a relationship with Him. This is impossible to do."

Everyone knows you can't get to know someone without spending time with him or her. Why is it, then, that so many Christians try to know and understand God without giving Him time to touch their hearts?

God longs to spend time with you. What a thought! The Lord of all creation wants to hang with you. The more time you spend with Him, the better you'll know Him. As your Teacher and Guide, He will develop your character to be like His own.

So how can you tell if this process is actually occurring in your life? You can start by taking a spiritual inventory:

- Are you growing in the knowledge of God's truth? In 1 Peter 2:2, God commands us to "crave pure spiritual milk, so that by it you may grow up in your salvation." God's truth, hidden in His Word, is the best nourishment for your character. Do you crave it and drink it in?

- Are you growing as a man or woman of prayer? In *The Weapon of Prayer,* E. M. Bounds states, "What the church needs today is not better machinery, not new organizations or more novel methods, but men whom the Holy Spirit can use—men of prayer.... He does not anoint plans, but men—men of prayer." Can the Holy Spirit use you as a man or woman of prayer?

- Are you in fellowship with other believers? If you're walking with Christ, you must have fellowship with others. "But if we walk in the light, as he is in the light, we have fellowship with one another, and the blood of Jesus, his Son, purifies us from all sin" (1 John 1:7).

- Are you pursuing God's kingdom above all else? One of my favorite verses is Matthew 6:33: "But seek first his kingdom and his righteousness, and all these things will be given to you as well." If you seek Him first, He will grant you abundant life. What has priority in your thinking—enjoying your own dating life or seeking the Lord's control over it? When you consider entering into any dating relationship, ask yourself whether dating that person will help or hinder your efforts to seek God first.

As you answer these questions, be honest with yourself. How is your walk with God? If you see an area that could use improvement, diligently follow your Teacher. You *can* become the man or woman of character God desires you to be.

DON'T JUST SIT THERE

I believe God has a prince or princess for almost everyone. After all, you're a son or daughter of the King, so it's only fitting that you marry someone of nobility and character. But God doesn't want you to wait for that person by just sitting around and daydreaming about Mr. or Ms. Right. As Greg Laurie writes in his book *On Fire*, "Our responsibility is to attend to our walk, seeking to be what He calls us to be."

God wants to build character in your heart, and your job is to let Him do it, no matter what it takes. (Character development isn't easy.) You must truly humble yourself to learn from God and to cleanse your relationships of old "barbarian" patterns. Then God can crown you as the prince or princess He wants you to be, and pronounce you ready for someone equally noble.

Fortunately, you don't have to wait until you've finished developing character to start dating. (Actually, you won't be "finished" until you get to heaven.) So how can you determine if you're ready? I firmly believe that as you wait on the Lord, remain in His Word, and pray fervently, He will show you when you're ready.

Meanwhile, remember that it's better to wait longer than to cut your character development short. If you're unsure, holding off for a while won't hurt you. Give God time, and He'll show you the next step.

CHARACTER FIRST

In the Bible, the story of Rebekah illustrates how the best things come to those who build character instead of just sitting around. In Genesis 24, we read about Abraham sending his servant to find a wife for Isaac, Abraham's son. After a long journey, the servant stops at a well, a place where he knows the women of the area gather.

There he notices Rebekah, who's come to draw water for her family. "The girl was very beautiful, a virgin" (Genesis 24:16). Having maintained her purity, Rebekah shines radiantly because of it.

Then the servant asks Rebekah for a drink. She could easily respond, "Get your own water, buddy!" Instead, with compassion and humility, Rebekah serves this complete stranger. She draws water not only for him, but for his camels as well. (This was no small task, considering how much camels drink; after all, they have those humps to fill.)

Then Rebekah tells him, "We have plenty of straw and fodder, as well as room for you to spend the night" (Genesis 24:25).

To this man in need, Rebekah offers all she has—her service, her strength, and her family's support. What a woman of character! Clearly she valued serving others above herself.

As Genesis 24 closes, Rebekah willingly leaves her parents' household to marry a man of quality and nobility. Her character has won her a prince, literally—for Abraham's son Isaac was to be the crown prince of many nations.

Rebekah had not been running around trying to find her prince. Instead she had busied herself with service and character development, actively preparing herself for whatever God had planned. God honored her choice by clearly revealing when it was time for her to pursue a romantic relationship. When she was presented with a quality opportunity to develop a relationship, she responded with joy. (Though you can be sure that if some lowlife scum had approached her, she would have refused.) Rebekah didn't shrink from the opportunity with Isaac, but welcomed it. After having worked on her character, she felt ready to share herself with someone special.

Rebekah was blessed because she had learned to do what God told her to do—to serve and obey. She had waited for God.

In *My Utmost for His Highest,* Oswald Chambers writes, "To wait is not to sit with folded hands, but to learn to do what we are told."

HARD WORK

While you're in the process of character development, you may choose to date casually. After you've worked hard on becoming a man or woman of godly character, you can then begin the hard work of pursuing a serious relationship. Yes, relationship development also takes work. The "instant relationship" is a myth—you can't expect immediate depth or trust. Any quality relationship requires time, energy, and investment.

The relationship commands in Ephesians 4:2-3 reflect this: "Be completely humble and gentle; be patient, bearing with one another in love. Make every effort to keep the unity of the Spirit through the bond of peace."

Make every effort! Quality relationships result from quality effort.

Here's another good reminder: "Be devoted to one another in brotherly love. Honor one another above yourselves" (Romans 12:10).

Devoted, it says. Devotion means wholehearted commitment. You must wholeheartedly commit to build any relationship with brotherly love and sacrifice.

Relationships are serious business, calling for serious investment and commitment. Don't try to shortcut the process.

Timing Is Everything

READY...OR NOT?

I had it all dreamed out.

At the same time I'd be finishing up my four-year commitment to youth ministry at First Evangelical Free Church of Fullerton, I'd also be completing my seminary education. How cool it would be, I thought, to graduate from seminary with a degree in my left hand and my new wife on my right arm.

The timing would be perfect. With school behind me for good, I could focus on ministry and marriage.

But as I entered that final year of study at Talbot Seminary and youth ministry at "EV Free" (as we called it), a major problem presented itself. When you want to get married, a romantic relationship is sort of a prerequisite—and I had no immediate interests.

I also knew I wasn't getting any younger, a fact that everyone else seemed to recognize as well. Not that I needed Rogaine or anything. Still, almost every conversation I had eventually turned to why I hadn't found someone yet.

That year was a time of transition for me as I stared into an uncertain future. Little did I know that at the same time, only a few miles away, another Christian faced a similar situation.

Jerusha Redford had graduated from college a year early (lucky for me; otherwise our paths wouldn't have crossed). Desiring to serve the Lord full time, she began looking into foreign missions. She just kind of assumed God wanted her to be a single missionary in Africa.

But what she really longed to be was a wife and mother, not an overseas missionary. While she investigated and prayed, she decided to get involved with youth ministry at her home church. That church just happened to be the one where I was on staff. (Again, lucky me!)

A few months earlier, my boss, Eric Heard, had told me Jerusha might be joining our high-school ministry staff. So I knew a little about her.

Actually, I knew a lot about her. Eric had filled my ear with talk of Jerusha and her family. And Dale, my senior pastor, once cornered me in the church lobby and spent almost half an hour telling me why I had to meet Jerusha Redford.

For weeks Dale kept asking if I'd taken her out yet. He also told Jerusha that he'd set someone on her trail. Jerusha didn't know if this was someone she wanted to meet or someone to avoid like the plague. Not that she distrusted Dale; she just didn't like the idea of being set up.

When we did meet, Jerusha and I clicked almost immediately. One Wednesday night after youth group, we spent two hours talking in a church parking lot in the freezing cold (or so she remembers it). She kept saying she should go, but she just never left.

From that time forward, Jerusha and I invested a lot of time in getting to know each other. Since she had finished college and I had completed the majority of my seminary education (including Greek and Hebrew—the most brutal of seminary tortures), we both had time for a serious relationship.

We also shared strong convictions about dating and our walk with Christ. We started and developed our relationship with clear intentions. We wanted to honor the Lord while we got to know each other.

Almost all our dates focused on conversation instead of activity. Our first date never went beyond the restaurant. We sat at the same table for hours that Friday night, barely noticing our waitress's frustrated attempts to clear us out. We had connected too well to care.

After dating a short while, we both realized we were ready to invest more. Our relationship progressed, and we continued to open up to each other. Eventually, I couldn't imagine life without her. I wanted her to stay by my side—forever.

Jerusha and I were ready to consider marriage. We were both finished with school. We had both dated enough to know what we wanted. We had both spent considerable time developing our character and our personal relationship with Christ. In God's timing, our seasons of life fit perfectly.

IN HIS TIME

I hope you understand that Jerusha and I weren't handed some exclusive deal for only the few. God's timing is always perfect for all His children—including you. "He has made everything beautiful in its time" (Ecclesiastes 3:11). God knows exactly what's down the road for you, and in His time He *will* fit everything together flawlessly.

"Everything" includes your dating relationships and your desire for marriage. If you give Him the time to do it, He'll make your relationships beautiful.

It's really all about patience. You must learn to wait on God's timing and trust that it is perfect—always! You must let Him prepare you for healthy relationships and show you what kind of dating you're ready for.

And that brings us to the three different stages of readiness for dating. Let's take a closer look at them.

READINESS STAGE ONE

Maybe you can relate to Anna's story. A beautiful fourteen-year-old, Anna attracted all kinds of stares. As a young woman committed to purity, however, Anna pursued her relationship with Christ first.

Then a good friend of her older brother started showing interest. Eighteen-year-old Derek came from a solid and respected Christian family. I knew both of them because they attended a Sunday night Bible study group that I led.

Anna's parents had clearly laid down the dating "law." She was not to date until sixteen, period. Her parents had seen Derek's interest and had asked Anna's brothers to keep them apart as much as possible. Anna knew her parents' desire, yet she felt drawn to Derek and flattered that he would show interest.

One Sunday, Anna's friend Rachel approached me in a panic. She couldn't find Anna anywhere. I asked Rachel where she had last seen Anna.

Rachel stared at the floor for a second, and I could see her struggling. Finally she told me she thought Anna might be in the parking lot with Derek. Red flags waved in my mind.

I stepped outside and spotted Derek's car. Sure enough, the two young people were sitting in the car, listening to CDs. I knocked on the window and asked them to come inside. Both quickly assured me they "weren't doing anything."

I had to disagree. No, they weren't kissing, but Anna knew that sitting alone in the parking lot during Bible study time was an off-limits activity. She knew her parents wouldn't approve and that she had acted in disobedience.

Colossians 3:20 states clearly, "Children, obey your parents in everything, for this pleases the Lord." There's no escape clause in there for dating. "Obey...in everything" means just what it says.

If your parents have told you dating isn't an option until a certain age, then it's not an option. Your only choices are to obey or disobey. Behind door number one, obedience wins you the favor of the Lord and your parents. Behind door number two, disobedience wins you the displeasure of both your parents and your God. Double whammy.

Obeying your parents is worthwhile. You may feel as if they're trying to hold you back or treat you unfairly. They're not. In fact, here are a few good reasons to obey your parents and wait for their approved time frame:

- In *Why Wait?* author Josh McDowell notes that students who begin dating before the age of sixteen are more likely to engage in premarital sexual activities than those who start dating at age sixteen or later. Hello! That should be reason enough to wait. But there's more...

- In the survey I conducted, an overwhelming number of students believed that one-on-one dating should begin at age sixteen or older. These are your peers and your friends. Let's face it: If your parents, Christian leaders, and your friends agree on something, it's probably a good idea.

- If you obey and wait, you won't have to sneak around or lie. Deceit is always sinful. If you think you'll be happy sneaking around until you're old enough to date openly, you're wrong. The more you lie, the more trapped you'll become.
- If you wait and obey, you'll have time to focus on character development. You'll be able to discover who God wants you to be as well as the sort of people He wants you to develop relationships with. Then, when your parents say you're old enough, you'll be ready to date to His glory.

You may feel ready to date now, but your parents have said no. If so, then you aren't ready. Just remember that anything worth having is worth waiting for.

READINESS STAGE TWO

Being allowed to date doesn't automatically mean you're ready for a serious relationship. In this second stage, you probably want to focus on casual dating relationships. These relationships can glorify God if you proceed with caution.

I've watched many young people crash and burn in this stage. They rush into a level of intensity that they're not ready for. They get too serious, too soon.

I remember watching two students struggle with this. Katie and Michael enjoyed each other's company. Their relationship took off, and they were soon spending a great deal of time together.

As they were finishing high school, however, a major disagreement emerged. It turned out that Katie assumed their relationship would end before they went to college. Unfortunately, Michael hadn't assumed the same thing. Even if they weren't ready for marriage, he wanted to keep things going. Thankfully the situation didn't get ugly, but as they broke up, both were hurt and confused. Without careful thinking, they had become too serious, too soon.

How can you evaluate whether you're becoming too serious, too soon? One surefire way is to use parents and friends as a barometer. If they question the amount or type of time you're spending in a relationship, you probably want to ease things up a bit.

You can also check your attitude when your boyfriend or girlfriend spends time with other people. If you start resenting the fact that she wants to go shopping on Saturday night or that he wants to watch the game with his buddies, you may want to rethink how serious you've become.

Remember, too, that high school generally isn't the time to enter into superserious, "I'd die without him (or her)" relationships. At this time in life, it's easy to believe you're ready for a deeper relationship when you really aren't. It's so easy to make the mistake of putting other important things in life on hold and to neglect your friends and family for the sake of a dating relationship.

If you find yourself getting serious too quickly, slow down! Your best defense is caution. If a relationship is going to work, it doesn't matter how slowly it progresses. Don't be in a hurry to get close. Instead, work to keep things appropriate for your stage of life.

If you've already gotten too serious, however, there are a few steps you can take immediately to slow things down. First, stop spending every free moment with your boyfriend or girlfriend. Develop and maintain your same-sex friendships and your family relationships.

You can also use the phone less. (There's a novel concept!) It will be easier to stay lighthearted in your relationship if you aren't on the phone together three hours every night.

Finally, make the focus of your dates fun, not romance. If your dates are all candlelight dinners and moonlight strolls, you may be getting more serious than you're ready for.

If you need to break up, that's okay; life will go on. But preventive medicine is always best. Aim to be lighthearted from the start, and you'll see the benefits of dating at a slower pace.

I like the way Oswald Chambers (in *My Utmost for His Highest*) defines *readiness:* "a right relationship to God and a knowledge of where we are at present." Did you catch those two parts to readiness? The first is knowing God; the second is knowing yourself and where you really are.

Your "right relationship" with God needs to be first priority. How did you rate on the spiritual inventory in the last chapter? Are there still some areas you should work on before you think about a serious dating relationship? If so, use the time when you casually date to prepare your heart.

Do you know where you are at present? Are you in a position to have a serious relationship? Do you have commitments to school, family, or activities that would limit your time to date? Be realistic about where you are.

Readiness and patience go hand in hand. Eventually you'll be ready for something more serious. For now, keep your dating relationships lighthearted. As you casually date, be patient and content. "Wait for the LORD; be strong and take heart and wait for the LORD" (Psalm 27:14).

READINESS STAGE THREE

Sometimes readiness for a serious commitment comes only after long periods of waiting and watching. To quote Oswald Chambers again, "There is a cloud on the friendship of the heart, and often even love itself has to wait in pain and tears for the blessing of fuller communion."

Darryl met Shannon the first day of Master's College orientation. It was love at first sight for Darryl, but Shannon didn't experience their introduction in the same way.

Darryl and I became close over the four years he pursued Shannon. I watched as he kept trying and trying and trying. Sometimes the other guys would give him a hard time, but that didn't seem to faze the man. He continued to pursue.

Always good friends, Darryl and Shannon had their share of D.T.R. (define the relationship) talks. According to Shannon, she loved their friendship but didn't want to ruin it. Round and round they went.

The summer after graduation, I thought the sky might fall. Darryl and Shannon officially started dating. No one but those two knew quite what had happened, but from what we could tell, graduation and the threat of separation made Shannon realize that she didn't want to live without Darryl.

It had taken four years for Darryl and Shannon to prepare for a serious commitment. They first needed to experience college life and to further develop their relationships with Christ. As they matured in Him, they longed more and more for a companion and a friendship of the heart.

Eventually Darryl and Shannon knew that their commitment was more intense than a casual dating relationship. All serious relationships differ from casual ones not only in intensity but also in purpose. Serious relationships are designed to move toward marriage. So you must carefully consider your own readiness for marriage as you ponder whether to move your casual dating to the next level.

Following are some good questions to ask yourself about your readiness for a serious relationship. They aren't necessarily black-and-white questions with yes-or-no answers, but they'll help you think through the core issues.

- *How content are you in your relationship with Christ?* Whenever I felt myself longing for a dating relationship, I'd first ask myself if something was missing in my walk with Jesus.

- *What is your motivation for a more serious relationship?* Do you just want to have fun, or do you want something more serious? Is the relationship about you or about the other person?

- *How well have you pursued your personal spiritual growth?* I'm not talking about just going to church. Have you gotten to know God on your own? Are you spiritually equipped to love another person as Christ would want you to?

- *Have you set physical and emotional boundaries for this relationship?* Have you seriously considered these boundaries and written them down? If you don't know your own limits, you aren't ready for a serious relationship.

- *Would others say you're ready?* Listen to your parents, your church leaders, your friends. Many times the Lord uses others to help us see what we cannot see on our own.

- *Do you have time for a serious relationship?* Serious relationships take a lot of time, energy, and investment. If you're consumed with school, career, or hobbies, you won't be able to truly honor a relationship.

As with all your concerns, take this issue of your readiness to the Lord in prayer. Ask Him to clearly reveal to you whether you're ready.

If you know you're *not* ready, ask Him to show you how to prepare yourself for a serious commitment later.

If you sense you *are* ready, or if you're already in a serious relationship, ask the Lord to reveal the next step. He will faithfully guide you.

A TIME FOR EVERYTHING

There once was a woman who received a cocoon as a gift. When the butterfly within began to poke through the tough outer shell, she dreamed of the beauty to come.

One day she noticed that the butterfly's struggle to free itself seemed quite slow and painful. With the best intentions, the woman decided to slice open the cocoon. The butterfly crawled out...and promptly died.

The woman hadn't realized that only the struggle and the waiting made the butterfly ready to be free. Without the proper amount of time, the butterfly could not survive.

Timing is everything.

"There is a time for everything, and a season for every activity under heaven" (Ecclesiastes 3:1). There is a time for obediently not dating, a time for casual dating, and a time for serious relationships.

Don't sidestep the prep time or try to "free" yourself. Instead, trust God to reveal what you're ready for. If you take Him at His word, you'll have the privilege of watching exactly *how* He makes all things beautiful in His time.

Compromising Who You Are for What You Want

MEDIOCRITY VERSUS EXCELLENCE

It was a classic case: boy and girl thrown together to spend countless hours on the same project.

Jesse began working closely with Rebecca in fifth-period journalism. He was a junior and she was a senior. Exactly when he noticed her striking eyes or brilliant smile, I'm not sure. But let me tell you how easy it was for Jesse to fall for this attractive non-Christian.

Jesse is a real person, a young man I had the opportunity to disciple for four years. Not only was Jesse a devout believer when he developed feelings for this woman of another faith, he was also a leader in the youth group and a role model for many. Jesse played electric guitar in the praise band, went on mission trips, and was known at school as a committed Christian. His family was devoted to worship and service, and his father worked in ministry.

Shouldn't he have known better? I thought he did.

Strong upbringing and even extensive knowledge of God's Word didn't stop Jesse from dwelling on the glances Rebecca shot his direction and the attractive way she carried herself. The fact that she showed interest, even flirted a little, exhilarated him and made him feel alive.

Jesse's friends noticed right away that sparks were flying. Since they were concerned about him, and especially about his walk with Christ, they warned him of the dangers involved in pursuing an unbeliever. Several times they confronted him, urging him not to further the relationship. As Jesse now recalls, he chose—deliberately and willfully—not to listen to them. He was enthralled with Rebecca's beauty, blinded by it. He thought he could handle the situation. His pride got in the way.

Despite the consistent warnings of his closest friends and my own rebuke, Jesse began to date Rebecca. Ignoring God's call on his life, Jesse "followed his heart" and got what he wanted. Though Jesse had secretly hoped and prayed that Rebecca would come to know Christ, he discovered that dating someone of another faith and living out his beliefs at the same time was simply impossible. Not only did he quickly find the relationship didn't satisfy, but it caused him to fall away from the Lord as well.

Jesse had compromised.

As I watched Jesse's slide, the whole situation totally baffled me. I'd spent hours and hours mentoring Jesse in his faith. I was angry and frustrated because one of my star students was willfully disobeying the Lord. It felt like he was betraying me.

When I stepped back and surveyed the situation, I recognized the work of the Evil One. Isn't it just like the enemy to trick us into thinking we've got it all together and that we could never fall? Jesse was doing a lot of things right, but pride made him weak to temptation.

Jesse now admits that the differences in his and Rebecca's beliefs eventually caused a lot of tension. After six months, their dating spell ended in a terrible breakup. It was all unnecessary pain, he acknowledges.

Jesse now fully recognizes that he compromised who he was in order to get what he wanted. "She was just so beautiful," he remembers thinking, "and so special." Fortunately, Jesse never totally abandoned his Christian beliefs, but he did temporarily disregard them for momentary pleasure. "I wasn't really looking to the future," he later confessed. If he had, he added, he would have seen from the start that the relationship could never have worked.

WEAKNESS FOR WOMEN

Let's look at a story in the Bible about someone else who compromised for the same reasons that Jesse did.

Imagine being so exceptional that an angel announced your birth and gave your parents specific instructions for your life. Samson was such an individual. Not once, but twice an angel appeared to Samson's parents to tell them about him. They knew before he was even conceived that he would be a man "set apart to God from birth" as a leader for his people, helping the Israelites to throw off the oppressive Philistines (Judges 13:5).

The angel also announced that "no razor may be used on his head" (13:5). I'm sure that made for one incredibly long ponytail as Samson grew up.

Eventually Samson would become the "big man" in Israel. The Holy Spirit would rest upon him in strength. He would soon be the Israelite Terminator.

But first, puberty hit (uh-oh; we know what that means). Along with zits and the dreaded squeaky-voice syndrome, Samson began to experience all the emotions that go along with being a young man. He flirted with lust and sexual temptation. When Samson wandered into Timnah, a city only a few miles from his home, his eyes fell on a hot young Philistine woman, and he was consumed with the desire to have her.

Now God had been very clear about who the Israelites could and could not marry. Philistines were definitely off-limits. They worshiped false gods, offering human and sexual sacrifices. *Sick!* Samson knew God's laws—no doubt about it. But instead of choosing God's high standard, Samson followed his lustful heart and married the woman he saw in Timnah.

This marriage ended fast enough to make your head spin. Their belief systems contradicted each other completely, and ultimately she chose to do the Philistine thing, betraying Samson. You can read about it in the fourteenth chapter of Judges.

Unfortunately, Samson didn't learn his lesson. He just couldn't get over his Philistine fetish. In Judges 16 we read how he once again disobeyed God and allowed himself to fall in love with another Philistine woman named Delilah, who was even more dangerous than his first wife. Further down the slope of compromise he slipped.

Remember, Samson had been set apart by God to defeat the Philistines, and God's power rested upon him. Samson had carefully hidden the source of his strength—his uncut hair—from his Philistine enemies. Until, that is, Delilah deceived him into revealing his God-given secret. Once in her clutches, Samson lost not only his hair but also the blessing of the Holy Spirit.

The Philistines gouged out Samson's eyes before throwing him into prison to die. Humiliated by his own foolish choices, Samson eventually died from the consequences of his compromise.

Now I know you don't want your own story to be anything like this. So let's talk about what to watch out for.

THE MOMENTUM OF MEDIOCRITY

The first thing to avoid is the momentum of mediocrity. And if you don't know what mediocrity is, let me fill you in.

Mediocrity is what happens to people who settle for less than the best. A mediocre person becomes satisfied with the ordinary or the barely adequate. He or she could care less about excellence.

Compromise is the temptation to be mediocre—to stray from the ultimate standard of quality that God has given us and to settle for something cheap and shoddy instead.

Samson's story teaches us that compromise has a snowball effect. It creates downward momentum that thrusts us toward mediocrity. Instead of inspiring drive and determination, compromise makes laziness seem acceptable. It lets you off the hook, so to speak.

Compromise may begin with something as "small" as a lingering look, but as we've seen with Samson, it can end in death. Compromise spins a web of self-deceit and disregard for God that will eventually ensnare you. The momentum and force of mediocrity will take over.

THINKING YOU'RE SAFE

Sometimes compromise sneaks up on you even when you date a Christian. Let me tell you how it happened to me.

It was Christmas Day, and my parents dropped me off at the airport for my return to seminary and youth ministry work. Everything looked normal: Mom cried as usual when I said good-bye, and I was loaded down with luggage plus an oversized poster from the movie *Mars Attacks!* (a white elephant gift—gotta love those).

Boarding the plane, I noticed an attractive young woman. I shot up a little prayer to God: "Why can't I meet a girl like that, Lord?"

Well, that prayer got answered. That cute girl was my flight attendant, Kourtney, and because the plane was pretty empty, she had plenty of time to chat. Before my second bag of peanuts, I discovered that Kourtney had a relationship with Christ and that we lived close to each other. I was stoked. I liked this immediate answer-to-prayer thing.

Kourtney gave me her phone number (plus another round of peanuts) and walked with me off the plane. We started dating, and two weeks later she was telling me that she loved me and that I was "the one." She was already planning the wedding.

Hold up, I thought. She was cool and all, but I didn't really know her. Her intensity swept me up, though, and we got pretty serious.

Don't get me wrong. Kourtney was a great girl who loved the Lord. But we were on different pages. Actually I think we were in different books altogether. I was serious about ministry, but our relationship was completely separate from that part of my life. Kourtney didn't have time to get involved with my commitment to the church. I felt as if I was letting our relationship pull me away from seminary, from my students, and from my intimacy with the Lord. I knew it had to stop. But I really liked her, and it was hard to break up.

Kourtney and I split up in early spring, and that summer I took a team of students to Poland for a two-month mission trip. The time away from her confirmed that we didn't complement each other. In fact, we had compromised to be together.

By dating a Christian I thought I could stand strong, but I realized I needed to be in a relationship that challenged me to meet my life's goals. I needed to be with someone who shared my heart for ministry and for service.

RISKY BUSINESS

Obviously, relationships are risky business. Samson really fell on his face because of a woman, and Jesse and I both found out that dating without careful consideration can quickly distract you from what should be your first priority.

So what does all this talk about compromise really teach us?

- First, it demonstrates the power of love and relationships, and that relationships with the opposite sex are a potential danger zone. As the Song of Songs expresses it, "Love is as strong as death.... Many waters cannot quench love; rivers cannot wash it away" (8:6-7). The fires of passion will burn us if we leave our hearts unguarded. The wounds of inappropriate relationships are severe and long-lasting.

- Second, these stories call us to stay alert. Temptations arising from relationships with the opposite sex will be powerful. We must guard against the enemy's subtle call to compromise. Satan always wants you to "settle," because unlike God our Father, he cares nothing for your happiness or fulfillment. God warns us to "be self-controlled and alert. Your enemy the devil prowls around like a roaring lion looking for someone to devour" (1 Peter 5:8).

- Finally, we see that complacency is hazardous to a Christian's health. When everything seems fine and the consequences of "small" compromises are not immediately evident, you may begin to feel invincible. Pride will tell you that you can handle anything. Jesse thought he could convert Rebecca and that dating her wouldn't really affect his future. Samson assumed he was strong enough to handle Delilah and that he could marry an enemy. And I thought that since Kourtney was a Christian, our relationship was safe. I found myself unaware, complacent, and proud.

Pride will always lie to you. It will convince you that you're unshakable. Trust me, you're not! "If you think you are standing firm, be careful that you don't fall!" (1 Corinthians 10:12). Let us never pridefully trust in our own strength or wisdom, for the dangers of dating relationships are real and serious.

Every aspect of your relationships matters to God. Maybe you think that it's nothing to be concerned about if your relationships don't quite meet God's standard, since you aren't involved in "big sins" like going all the way. Don't be fooled—small sins don't stay small. God reminds us of this in Romans 6:19, where He warns about offering our bodies "to ever-increasing wickedness." He tells us to instead offer our bodies "to righteousness leading to holiness." Are you offering your body to righteousness? Or are you compromising who you are for what you want?

GETTING WHAT YOU WANT
WITHOUT COMPROMISE

Let's think about it now in terms of your destiny—your God-determined course for life.

When you became a child of God, He sealed you with the Holy Spirit (Ephesians 1:13-14). As my mentor, Eric Heard, used to say, it's "God in your bod." He is your guide and counselor. You are not alone in your dating relationships. You have the Spirit of the living God dwelling within you!

So many times we underestimate or downplay the importance of this fact. But this is HUGE—God is inside you! He's always there to let you know what to do. You don't have to wonder about it; just ask for His help. He promises to give you wisdom to live according to His will and to resist the temptation to compromise.

Remember, the Lord wants (and provides) the absolute best for your life. Through His Spirit within you He equips you with love, joy, peace, patience, kindness, goodness, faithfulness, gentleness, and self-control (Galatians 5:22-23). He also wants to give you a mate of noble character, someone worthy of the prince or princess that you are. (You may feel like only a frog right now, but give it some time.)

You're building a strong foundation for achieving this destiny! You're learning how to act like royalty by spending time with the King in Bible study, prayer, and fellowship with other believers. In the secure knowledge of your position in Christ, you can keep falling more deeply in love with God, allowing Him to develop your character. After all, you and I are "set apart" for God every bit as much as Samson was.

Samson blew it, but you and I don't have to. Fortunately the Bible records not only the stories of those who compromised, but also the examples of those who didn't.

SUCCESS STORY

Remember the Old Testament story of Joseph, the boy whose brothers sold him into slavery? Joseph became a godly Hebrew man who by God's grace found himself (in Genesis 39) managing the household of Potiphar, one of Egypt's military leaders. Potiphar trusted him with everything he owned. Joseph even got to drive Potiphar's BMW chariot.

"Joseph was well-built and handsome," the passage tells us, and Potiphar's wife wanted him in the worst way. Day after day she tried to seduce him, and "day after day [Joseph] refused to go to bed with her or *even be with her*" (39:6,10, emphasis added). That's what I call a man of no compromise!

One day Potiphar's wife went too far. She cornered Joseph and threw herself at him. When he refused her again, she grabbed hold of him. This chick wouldn't take no for an answer. Joseph fled so quickly that he was forced to leave his cloak in her clutches. Rejected and burning with anger, Potiphar's wife deceived her husband into believing that Joseph had taken advantage of her.

As a result, Joseph ended up spending years in Egypt's Alcatraz. Yet he continued to trust God even in prison, and through an incredible series of events (as told in Genesis 40–41), Joseph became Pharaoh's right-hand man, overseeing all of Egypt. That's quite a switch: prisoner to prime minister. God exalted him because Joseph had chosen not to compromise. The Lord gave him more than he could ever have imagined, let alone wanted!

Joseph lived a life of obedience and excellence. He resisted the temptation to be mediocre, and God blessed his decisions. By adhering to God's ultimate standard, Joseph got it all.

That can be the story of your life as well. You can live an uncompromising life the way Joseph did. By refusing to give in to sin, you'll reap the benefits of God's blessing.

Will you choose to live like Joseph? Or will you settle for less than God's best?

Whatever you want right now cannot compare to what God

wants for you. Don't compromise who you are just because someone is attractive or interested in you. Don't settle for mediocrity, which can never be fulfilling. Look to your future, to the destiny of greatness and adventure God has in store for you. Know who you are, and never lose sight of it for any momentary desire.

The excellent lies before you. Why would you choose anything else?

Defending
the Emotional Zone

GUARDING YOUR HEART

Earlier I mentioned a two-month mission trip to Poland that I took one summer. Twenty-four high-school seniors made up the mission team, and joining me in leading the group were two married couples plus another single (like myself at the time).

The other single leader, Kathleen, was well respected by students and adults alike. Kathleen exemplified a heart devoted to God and His people. She loved ministering to students, and they enjoyed her. Her intelligence and conversation skills impressed me. This woman was quality.

For several months before the trip, as well as each day in Poland, Kathleen and I spent quite a bit of time together. When we returned from Poland, we continued to hang out. We no longer *had* to, but we chose to anyway.

I wondered more than once if I should date her. We had shared so much. But I had never had "feelings" for Kathleen. It just didn't seem right. Even recognizing all her great character traits, I didn't see us together.

Things came to a head when I had an emergency tonsillectomy. In my vulnerable state, Kathleen served me by taking me home from the hospital, going to the store to buy Jell-O (the only food I could barely squeeze down), and hanging out at my place when I was the worst possible company.

Gradually it hit me: Kathleen and I were acting like a couple. We'd never so much as held hands, but we might as well have been dating. We had emotionally bonded. Our relationship had become intimate whether we would have admitted it or not.

Though nothing physical had happened, our relationship had entered a zone of emotional intimacy. Before Poland we had talked about guidelines in our relationship; now we'd allowed ourselves to overstep those boundaries.

Because I didn't intend to date her, our emotional closeness was inappropriate. I knew I had to take responsibility for having broken the boundaries we'd set. Kathleen and I talked. Both of us agreed that things needed to change, so we backed off from the relationship. Thankfully, I can tell you that we remained friends, but it was painful to break the emotional bonds we had forged.

WHY WE WANT INTIMACY

Intimacy—the personal closeness of a relationship—arises when two people share their lives, either through mutual experience or through conversation.

We all long for intimacy to some degree. As Cynthia Heald writes in *Intimacy with God,*

> There is a restlessness deep within each of us that compels us to search for the person, the place, the job, the "god" that will fill the void and give us peace. This restlessness essentially becomes a pursuit to find someone who will love us for who we are, understand our fears and anxieties, [and] affirm our worth.

We crave emotional intimacy because we all want to be known and to be loved.

Emotional intimacy is wonderful. Intimacy between men and women is especially wonderful because though men and women are so different, they complement one another. Yet inappropriate intimacy between a man and woman can be painful. Emotional intimacy should be reserved for certain times and relationships. That's why you must protect yourself and others by setting boundaries for your emotional zone.

Having emotional boundaries doesn't mean refusing to get close to anyone. But it does mean you wisely recognize that sharing yourself too quickly, or without even knowing it, can set you up for serious pain that's both unhealthy and unnecessary.

WHY YOU NEED BOUNDARIES

In the dating survey I conducted, I asked students if they had established emotional boundaries. Many young people had trouble answering that question. One eighteen-year-old's response sums up the confusion: "I don't really know what that means."

Quite simply, a boundary sets limits. I'm sure you've heard how important it is to set limits on your physical relationship (a topic we'll hit in a later chapter). It's just as essential to guard your emotions.

You can share almost all of yourself without ever holding hands. When you let someone into your heart and soul, you become intimate. You give part of yourself to that person.

If you're still wondering why it's imperative that you develop emotional boundaries, let me give you my top five reasons:

1. *God commands it.* In Proverbs 4:23 the Lord tells us, "Guard your heart, for it is the wellspring of life." Intimacy involves the heart. Your "heart" refers to all that you are—your personality and the depths of your soul. It's the source of your very life! So God commands you to watch over it vigilantly. The best way to stand guard over your emotional zone is to set clear boundaries and let no one trespass. For example: Jerusha and I decided from the beginning that we wouldn't tell each other "I love you" unless we were engaged to be married. We wanted to guard the true meaning of those words.

2. *Inappropriate intimacy can burn you.* Emotional ties are sometimes harder to break than physical ones. If you create strong emotional bonds with someone and then break up, the separation can be nasty and heart wrenching. Imagine if you gave a precious gift to an irresponsible person. He or she would probably break it—or at least not appreciate it. In the same way, if you give the treasure of yourself to someone unworthy or unprepared, you will get hurt.

3. *Inappropriate intimacy now can take away from appropriate intimacy later.* What you choose to do with emotional boundaries now can either protect or harm your future marriage. I made one of my greatest mistakes when I was a senior in high school. I dated the same girl for over a year, and we shared almost everything. Let me tell you, I wish I had been more careful. Our inappropriate intimacy later burned me when I shared the details of that relationship with Jerusha.

4. *Boundaries protect you from the world.* The world doesn't share

Christ's vision of intimacy, and it will try to ensnare you with bad advice. The voices of the world will tell you, "You never lose by loving. You always lose by holding back" (Barbara De Angelis); "It's all right letting yourself go, as long as you can get yourself back" (Mick Jagger). Don't be fooled by this phony wisdom. You *will* lose by loving before you're ready, and you can't take back memories or shared experiences. The Lord tells us to protect our soul from the lies of the world. "In the paths of the wicked lie thorns and snares, but he who guards his soul stays far from them" (Proverbs 22:5). Setting boundaries will help you stay far from the world.

5. *Only God can truly fill your love void.* So often we expect human love to meet the needs we have for intimacy, but people will disappoint you more often than not. God alone loves perfectly and always. He tells us, "Though the mountains be shaken and the hills be removed, yet my unfailing love for you will not be shaken" (Isaiah 54:10). When you're full of the unfailing love of God, you'll need and expect less of the imperfect love that comes from human beings.

WHERE TO DRAW THE BOUNDARIES

How exactly do you develop these emotional limits? The following practical recommendations will help you draw the boundaries.

Decide ahead of time. If you set emotional boundaries before you begin a relationship, you'll be more likely to stick to them. You can follow the example of Isaiah, who wrote, "Because the Sovereign LORD helps me, I will not be disgraced. Therefore have I set my face like flint, and I know I will not be put to shame" (Isaiah 50:7). Because of his predecision to be as unyielding as a rock, Isaiah knew he would not experience shame. You will never have to be ashamed of your relationships if you set unyielding boundaries and honor them with your actions. More importantly, as Isaiah pointed out, you will have the help of the Lord.

Ask for guidance. The Bible instructs us, "If any of you lacks wisdom, he should ask God, who gives generously to all without finding fault, and it will be given to him" (James 1:5). Ask God to give you wisdom about what you should and should not share with another person. Spend time in prayer, asking Him to show you where you've been inappropriate in the past and how you can better guard your heart in the future. If you've earnestly sought His guidance, God will reveal where you should set your emotional boundaries.

Write down your boundaries. Think through what you want to save for marriage and then write down everything that comes to your mind. Maybe you'll decide you don't want to say "I love you" to anyone but your husband or wife. Whatever the boundary is, writing it down will make it more real and attainable.

Ask someone you trust to hold you accountable. Go to a parent, a leader at church, or a friend (of the same sex) and ask this person to look over your commitments and hold you accountable to them. Make sure you're willing to let this person ask you hard questions. When you start dating, be honest with your accountability partner about everything you share with your date. (Accountability works only if you're completely honest and willing to listen to someone else's counsel.) A faithful accountability partner can often recognize—more quickly than you can—when you're breaking the emotional boundaries you've set for yourself.

Communicate your boundaries. Make sure that anyone you date knows your limits. You can communicate these boundaries by stating them directly as well as by your example. If you're just beginning to develop a friendship or dating relationship with someone, steer the conversation toward topics that allow you to get to know him or her without emotionally attaching yourself to that person. Talk about the music he listens to or the books she reads instead of whether Hawaii or Europe is a better place for a honeymoon. If the other person brings up something intimate that crosses your boundaries, you can respond by saying you don't feel comfortable talking about that subject. It may be tough, but it will be worth the effort to prevent the greater pain later on of trying to break emotional bonds.

Choose wisely what to talk about. Some subjects are automatically more intimate than others. For the most part, marriage, sex, sin, and your "deepest secrets" should be off-limits. Maybe you think talking about marriage and kids is a joke, but you can never be sure whether the other person is on the same page. Pray the words of Psalm 141: "Set a guard over my mouth, O LORD; keep watch over the door of my lips" (verse 3).

Don't talk too much; focus instead on being a good listener. "Everyone should be quick to listen, slow to speak" (James 1:19). The more you listen, the less you speak, which means you'll have less time to say something inappropriate that you'll later regret. (God tells us in Proverbs 10:19, "When words are many, sin is not absent, but he who holds his tongue is wise." Think about it.) Besides, listening, rather than talking, is the best way to learn more about the other person.

Recognize when you've stepped over the line. Ask God to convict you whenever you go beyond a boundary. Have that request in mind as you regularly review the list of boundaries you've written down. In reviewing your list, you may realize that you've crossed one of the lines you've established. If the Spirit convicts you of this, change the course of your actions.

Instead of leaving your emotional boundaries to chance, seriously pray and consider how to set good limits. Recognize first that God can and will fill your needs for intimacy, then ask Him to teach you how to be appropriately intimate with others. Once you've set your boundaries, watch yourself closely, speak with care...and enjoy healthy levels of intimacy.

Getting Ahead of Yourself

Did Somebody Say "Marriage"?

Do you recall having seen the word *marriage* pop up anywhere in this book?

I'm sure you do. For example, when we looked at the different stages of readiness for dating, I mentioned that "serious relationships are designed to move toward marriage." And just in the last chapter I wrote, "What you choose to do with emotional boundaries now can either protect or harm your future marriage."

I obviously have marriage in mind as we look together at dating.

So it's time to make something clear. I believe there's a definite danger in becoming too marriage-conscious in a dating relationship. (This is probably even more of a hazard if you've been taught that you should date only if you're ready for marriage.) That's why we need to keep in focus a very important guideline that I've mentioned before: the need to stay lighthearted in your approach to dating.

The goals of a dating relationship should be to honor God while you get to know another person and, yes, to develop the skills eventually needed in marriage. To a certain extent it *is* healthy to think about marriage while dating. And certainly as you mature, your relationships will become more serious. No matter how old you are, however, you still need to maintain healthy emotional boundaries.

Marriage itself should not be the only target in sight as you date. You have to learn to view each dating relationship as a step in learning and growing.

PLAYING MARRIED

One of the ways this principle is violated is when couples "play married" even though they're only dating. Without ever saying "I do" and tying the knot, they pretend that their lives are already bound together with a husband-and-wife intensity.

You've probably seen examples of this—couples spending every possible moment together, opening a joint bank account, making a big purchase together. Or maybe the girl even does the guy's laundry. These things inevitably open up new levels of commitment and intimacy as the couple loses sight of the current reality of their relationship.

Single people should act differently than married people do. We read in 1 Corinthians 7 that the husband and wife belong to each other. Married people own each other to a certain extent. This is never the case with two single people in a relationship.

When single people play married, they selfishly act as if they own each other. As a result, possessive and demanding attitudes often flare up. People consumed with marriage often have fixed ideas about how the relationship should progress. They can become unreasonable, demanding that things go their way or not at all.

If you focus on playing married, you'll most likely develop an obsessive or possessive attitude that's damaging and that will overstep healthy emotional boundaries.

Of course, at a certain point in your dating life—when the time and season are right—the possibility of marriage will become an option, and you can begin focusing on it more clearly. Yet even then you must be careful to stay away from playing married.

THE ONE?

Besides questions about maintaining physical purity, the issue of "How will I know when I've found THE ONE?" seems to be the biggest concern about dating that I've encountered among young people. In a different manner, this represents another way in which marriage can become an unhealthy preoccupation while you're dating.

Wouldn't it be great if there were some automatic signal to show us the right person to marry? When I first met Jerusha, I would have appreciated a neon sign flashing over her head with the message, "YOU CAN STOP LOOKING NOW—THIS IS THE ONE!" However, as you can well imagine, that wasn't how things happened.

In fact, I struggled for years trying to determine how I would identify The One. I constantly questioned whether the girls I dated were "God's will for my life." And all the time I wondered if there really was just one person—one person alone—who was right for me.

I've become convinced that getting wrapped up in finding the one person who's right for you can damage your relationships. It can take your focus off Christ and place it on yourself. If you're consumed with knowing whether or not a person is The One, you may break emotional boundaries trying to find out. In your intense search, you may also drag a relationship beyond its natural course.

This happened to me when I dated a girl named Katie. When I first started dating Katie, everything seemed to click. We shared a passion for Christ, we both enjoyed working with students, and we had a lot fun together. We just hit it off.

As our relationship developed, many people began asking those "So...?" kinds of questions. I have to admit that I was asking them too. My best friends seemed all too ready to pronounce that Katie was God's will for me. Was she? I wanted to know. But I couldn't find a concrete way to decide for sure.

I thought it might clarify things if I took Katie to meet my family. At this point we'd been dating for several months. I wanted my family to know this girl I spent so much time with and to give me input about her.

My parents enjoyed her company and thought well of her, but they didn't ask me when to plan for the wedding. In fact, for Katie and me that visit home was heavy-laden with fights and heated moments.

As time went on, Katie and I argued more and more. Both of us have confrontational personalities, so we butted heads quite a bit. We disagreed on some major issues.

We started seeing that our passions and visions differed significantly. We didn't seem to be running in the same direction. Our communication became aggressive and intense instead of easygoing and respectful.

Our relationship hit a dead end. We saw clearly that we didn't click as well as we'd initially thought. We just weren't right for each other. Over time, God's will had crystallized regarding our relationship: It wasn't meant to go deeper.

KNOWING GOD'S WILL

As Christians we're encouraged to seek the will of God, and that's certainly true when it comes to dating and marriage. But if you're like I was, it's sometimes easy to take the wrong approach. The idea of finding God's will can actually become an oppressive concept if it's misunderstood.

In a powerful book entitled *Found: God's Will,* John MacArthur Jr. explains a common misconception about understanding the will of God:

> Some apparently think that God's will is lost. At least they say they are searching for it! To them, God must appear to be a sort of divine Easter bunny who has stashed His will, like eggs, somewhere out of sight and sent us running through life trying to find it.

God hasn't sent us on a search for the needle of His will in the haystack of life. He doesn't want you consumed with trying to find the one and only person to love and marry any more than He wants you to focus too intently on the one and only college to enroll in after high school or the one and only job to take after college.

"What one needs to know about the will of God," MacArthur writes, "is clearly revealed in the pages of the Word of God." He shows how we discover in Scripture that God's will is simply that we be (1) saved; (2) filled with His Spirit, through studying His Word; (3) pure—sanctified and holy; (4) obedient; and (5) humble, even in suffering.

MacArthur explains these five principles, then makes a radical statement about determining God's will for other aspects of life: "If you are doing all five of [these] basic things…do whatever you want! If those five elements of God's will are operating in your life, who is running your wants? God is!"

I'm not convinced that in God's will there's only one potential candidate to become your marriage partner for life. There are many God-fearing young men or women who would make a wonderful mate for you. What I am convinced of is this: *God's will is that you become the person He desires,* and not that you become obsessed with your search for The One.

You see, God doesn't want us to view His will as leading to a certain place or person. His will leads us to *be* a certain person, the son or daughter He wants to spend eternity with.

"Knowing God's will," MacArthur states, "may mean pushing down a narrow line until you hit a dead end." If you're truly obedient to these five principles of devotion to God, you may simply need to proceed in a dating relationship until it's obvious that you've hit a dead end. That's what happened with Katie and me. God's will became clear as time progressed.

Once you take your eyes off your search for The One, you'll be better equipped to recognize what kind of person God intends you to be. At that point, whoever you choose to marry will be God's will, because you'll be following Him first.

LOVING BY THE LIST

You've probably heard someone encourage you to make a list of the qualities and traits you desire in a future husband or wife. I believe making such a list is important and helpful. But if a person's list becomes a nonnegotiable standard, it may cause him or her to become judgmental and picky. This type of person develops an all-or-nothing mentality that says, "If you don't meet my require-ments, you're not worth my time."

I have a good friend back in California who's like that. He's a solid Christian man who's still single. Whenever I mentioned any particular young woman in our church and encouraged him to date her, his response was always "She's too this" or "She's not that." I got the impression that only a combination of Barbie and Mother Teresa could have fulfilled all his demands. Perhaps he needed to surrender some of the items on his list.

Perhaps you do too. If your list targets "a guitar-playing, poetry-writing, six-foot champion-surfer supermodel," I can almost guaran-tee you'll be disappointed in everyone you meet.

Determine what's negotiable and what isn't on your list. Maybe you've always wanted someone with blond hair, blue eyes, and a per-petual tan, but is all that really nonnegotiable?

Some things *should* be nonnegotiables on your list, such as a long and constant walk with Christ, a heart for the lost, and compassion. But surface traits and characteristics should never become essentials.

Don't allow a list of surface traits to control you. You'll miss out on a lot of opportunities to grow and be stretched by God's people.

By the way, here are a few items from my wife's list for her mate: stability, leadership, intensity, flexibility, peacemaker, responsibility, knowledge of God's Word, family-oriented, and proven track record of walking with the Lord. (Now you know how you can pray for me; I have a lot to live up to!)

GROW WISE BY STAYING HUMBLE

If you keep your dating focus too much on playing married, on find-ing The One, or on matching your overlong list of future-spouse requirements, your relationships can become static and shallow as you shut out of your life everyone who doesn't measure up to your expectations. Those approaches to dating should never become the central focus of your life. In fact, dating itself should not become the central focus of your life.

Dating should be a healthy means of personal growth for you, allowing you to develop your relationship skills and to prepare for the future in a way that honors God.

I believe it all comes down to a question of humility. If you have a humble and open heart, God will teach you all that you need to know as you date. So allow Him to make all the details clear in His time. Trust Him with where you are at present as well as for your future.

The Physical Fence

How Far Is Too Far?

That's what you really want to know, isn't it? *In the physical arena, how far is too far?* When I asked students for their number one question about dating, this was by far the most popular response.

I also found that there are many misconceptions about how to set and maintain physical boundaries for sexual purity. Some people wanted to avoid making decisions about sexual standards, some wanted to "play it by ear," and some even asserted that the Bible doesn't really speak clearly to this issue.

One fifteen year-old female claimed, "I don't think I'm ready to make those decisions."

WRONG!

Even if you're not dating, you need to make decisions *now* about your sexual purity. If you're old enough to even think about dating, you should be making choices about how you will stand for purity.

Several young men and women responded, "I will do what I feel comfortable doing."

WRONG AGAIN!

You may feel "comfortable" doing far more than God would approve of. Any sexual activity—from kissing to intercourse—may "feel good" or "seem right." But you need to make decisions based on conformity to God's standards, not on your own feelings or comfort level.

A seventeen-year-old junior even insisted that "there's nothing in the Bible" on this topic, "except about going all the way."

WRONG, WRONG, WRONG!

When it comes to sexual standards, the Bible talks about a lot more than just intercourse. If you assume that purity simply means refraining from "going all the way," you've missed God's message. He desires holiness and purity from your whole heart, soul, mind, and body.

THE WRONG QUESTION

No matter what the subject, asking the wrong question will always get you the wrong answer. I believe there's no way you'll discover God's perfect will for sexual purity by asking the question, "How far is too far?" If you're really trying to pursue purity, you can't start with a question that presupposes stretching the limits.

Let me explain. The Christian life isn't about living as close as possible to the edge of immorality. It's about living as close as possible to Jesus Christ. So, for a young man or woman who's intent on living purely, the ultimate question should be "How pure can I be?"

In this chapter, I'm not going to tell you whether or not kissing is right. I don't believe that's the essential point. The essential point is choosing whether you will stand for purity or for pleasure.

In 1 Peter 1:13-15 we find this challenge from God:

> Therefore, prepare your minds for action; be self-
> controlled; set your hope fully on the grace to be
> given you when Jesus Christ is revealed. As obedient
> children, do not conform to the evil desires you had
> when you lived in ignorance. But just as he who
> called you is holy, so be holy in all you do.

The holiness of God is the standard to which we're called. Asking a question like "How far is too far?" won't get you even close to that standard. If you're willing, however, to look at this chapter with the mind-set of how pure you can be, I believe God will reveal to you His standards for your personal purity.

HOW CLEAR IS THE BIBLE?

Most young Christians agree that God's Word teaches that sex should be reserved for marriage. I don't think most of them understand, however, that what God means by *sex* is much more than "going all the way."

I wasn't shocked to hear many students saying the Bible is unclear about sexual standards except premarital intercourse. This is a common misperception, and it originates in a lie of the Enemy.

Satan often deceives people into believing God's Word isn't clear when it comes to specifics. As long as the Enemy can make you believe that God's will in the area of sexual purity is gray or impossible to determine, he's got you right where he wants you—in the dark!

The Bible does shed light on the specifics of sexual purity. In His Word, God speaks out against all forms of sexual immorality and sexual impurity.

The Greek word for sexual impurity is *porneia*. God uses this word fifty-five times in the New Testament to describe prostitution, unchastity, fornication, and acts caused by lust.

Porneia is an umbrella term that covers all kinds of sexual filth, not just "going all the way." Just as the term "trash" can be applied to every type of garbage, *porneia* is any sexual activity that pollutes your purity. As John MacArthur points out in *Found: God's Will,* in order to remain pure, "we must not get involved in sexual acts that are wrong."

What are "sexual" acts? Sexual acts can be kissing, touching (let's get rid of that '70s word "petting"), oral sex, and so on, all the way to intercourse. Sexual acts include talking about and dwelling on sex. The simple entertaining of thoughts and fantasies about sex can be a sexual act.

When it comes to sexual purity, God is interested in the big picture. He wants you to avoid all *porneia,* a word which Eugene Peterson in *The Message* translates as "sexual promiscuity" (see 1 Thessalonians 4:3).

People usually think of promiscuity as having sex before marriage. Actually, promiscuity is any haphazard or thoughtless sexual behavior. It could include failing to decide your sexual standards ahead of time. It could include doing "whatever feels right." Promiscuity results from the thoughtless assumption that God is displeased only if you "go all the way." But God has commanded us to avoid promiscuity in every way.

FOR ALL THE RIGHT REASONS

If you still aren't convinced that God wants you to avoid all *porneia,* turn to 1 Corinthians 6:15–7:2. This is one of the most striking passages on sexual purity in the Bible. I love the way Eugene Peterson renders it in *The Message*, making its truth so tangible. I've used my own headings below to divide this passage into five parts, each with its own powerful reason for why Christians should flee from all sexual immorality:

Sexual acts are more than just physical.

> There's more to sex than mere skin on skin. Sex is as much spiritual mystery as physical fact. As written in Scripture, "The two become one."

Sexual acts outside of a marital commitment leave you lonely.

> Since we want to become spiritually one with the Master, we must not pursue the kind of sex that avoids commitment and intimacy, leaving us more lonely than ever....

Your body wasn't made for sexual sin.

> There is a sense in which sexual sins are different from all others. In sexual sin we violate the sacredness of our own bodies, these bodies that were made for God-given and God-modeled love, for "becoming one" with another.

Your body is not your own.

> Or didn't you realize that your body is a sacred place, the place of the Holy Spirit? Don't you see that you can't live however you please, squandering what God paid such a high price for? The physical part of you is not some piece of property belonging to the spiritual

part of you. God owns the whole works. So let people see God in and through your body.

Marriage is the only context for sexual acts.

Now, getting down to the questions you asked....
First, is it a good thing to have sexual relations?
Certainly—but only within a certain context. It's good for a man to have a wife, and for a woman to have a husband. Sexual drives are strong, but marriage is strong enough to contain them and provide for a balanced and fulfilling sexual life in a world of sexual disorder.

For all these reasons, God wants you to avoid sexual sin. God created all sexual activity to be celebrated and protected by the strong bonds of marriage. Outside of marriage, any sexual activity that leads to lust is *porneia* and must be avoided.

WHY YOU NEED BOUNDARIES

Both emotional and physical boundaries protect you from premature intimacy, and the reasons you should have physical limits are almost identical to the reasons we discussed for having emotional limits:

1. *God commands it.* We've just seen this, especially in our study of 1 Corinthians 6:15–7:2. Another clear passage is 1 Thessalonians 4:3: "It is God's will that you should be sanctified: that you should avoid sexual immorality."

2. *Inappropriate intimacy can burn you.* It will eventually destroy your relationships, either quickly or slowly. If you don't believe me,

ask someone who's experienced the painful consequences and regret of impure sexual activity. Those consequences can include pregnancy or sexually transmitted diseases. And guess what? It *can* happen to you. As the old saying goes, if you play with fire, you'll get burned.

3. *Inappropriate intimacy now can take away from appropriate intimacy later.* Physical intimacy before marriage will be a source of deep regret or much worse when the right time for intimacy comes—after your wedding. With each decision you make for purity, you "save yourself" for marriage. And consider this: Whatever you do before marriage, you will have to share with your future mate. Imagine having to tell him or her *everything.* Do you want to tell your husband that other men have seen you naked? Would you want to tell your wife you've had oral sex? Make decisions now that will help you avoid painful situations in the future.

4. *Boundaries protect you from the world.* The world's lies about physical intimacy seem to grow louder and stronger all the time. They're everywhere in our culture, and you desperately need boundaries to help you resist them.

5. *God alone can give the love you're looking for.* God is the One who created everything about your physical makeup, including your sexual drive. Only He knows completely how to best fulfill your needs, so you have every reason to trust Him in this area as in all others.

God's Word speaks forcefully about sexual boundaries. He says that living purely "means killing off everything connected with [the] way of death: sexual promiscuity, impurity, lust, doing whatever you feel like whenever you feel like, and grabbing whatever attracts your fancy. That's a life shaped by things and feelings instead of by God" (Colossians 3:5, *The Message*).

That phrase "killing off" is pretty intense, but it's there for a reason: God wants you to stay as far away as possible from sexual immorality of any kind. And to stay as pure as you can, you need to set physical boundaries that will protect you from falling into an inappropriate physical relationship. As a sixteen-year-old guy worded it on the survey, boundaries make sure "you don't even go down the path of lust."

AROUSAL AWARENESS

A lot of young people try to avoid the issue of physical boundaries by claiming they don't know what leads to lust and what doesn't. That's a cop-out. You can and should know what sets you off.

God has graciously given us built-in warning signals. You know when you're "turned on," because your whole body tells you so. At times simply holding hands may be too much, because your desires go wild.

You can know your trigger points, and you can know when to stop. The question is, will you do it?

IT'S ALL IN YOUR MIND

Other misconceptions can arise if you focus your sexual standards too narrowly on touching. Some people think that if they adopt a "nothing below the neck" approach or "stop at kissing," their purity will remain intact. Others believe they can go as far as "heavy kissing" or "making out," but that should be the limit.

It's not enough to simply be aware of how touching arouses you. The truth is, touching is simply an outgrowth of something that starts in your mind's eye. Holding hands can either be a pure impulse to draw closer or it can be the first step in fulfilling the lustful desires of your mind.

To be as pure as you can be, avoid anything that awakens inappropriate desires in your mind. A great majority of impure thoughts begin with something you see. But even this can be controlled. A remarkable man of God named Job expressed it this way: "I made a covenant with my eyes not to look lustfully at a girl" (Job 31:1). Whether you're a man or a woman, you can make a similar covenant to avoid the lust in your mind that starts with your eyes.

Purity is not just about touching. It's about your mind and your heart. Purity concerns your whole lifestyle. So take an inventory of your mind and your lifestyle. Do the pictures hanging on your wall encourage lustful thoughts? Do you and your friends talk about sex in ways that make you long for something you can't have? What about the movies you see, the music you hear, and the books and magazines you read?

Get the dirt out of your life. Clean the trash out of your mind. The more purely you think, the more purely you will act.

SUCCESSFUL STRATEGIES

In *Point Man*, Steve Farrar says this about maintaining sexual purity: "I had to have a plan in place to defeat the temptation that comes to me through my eyes.... I must anticipate and determine how I will act before I ever get into a tempting situation." You and I are no different. Maintaining sexual purity is probably a bigger battle than you've imagined, and you need a plan. So let's look at the three most useful strategies for maintaining purity in thought and action.

1. *Have a way of escape.* In Scripture the Lord admonishes us to "resist the devil" (James 4:7) and to "stand your ground" (Ephesians 6:13). For all kinds of temptations, He commands us to oppose them by standing firm.

When it comes to sexual immorality, however, God tells us to run! "Flee from sexual immorality" (1 Corinthians 6:18). He knows that sexual drives are powerful, and He instructs us to get as distant from sexual temptation as we possibly can. When it comes, don't stay put and try to overcome it. Escape!

2. *Have a dating plan that sets you up for success.* If your dates are carefully planned ahead of time—what you'll do, where you'll go, and with whom—you'll be a lot more successful in the war for purity. As my friend Melanie put it, "No guy is going to attempt the octopus on you at Starbucks!" Well said.

Think about it. When you're in a Christian atmosphere, you tend to act in a godly manner. Likewise, if you're in a worldly atmosphere—watching sexually explicit movies or having inappropriate conversations—you'll most likely act in a manner that reflects those impure surroundings.

Some people wonder with regret how they ended up "going so far" in physical intimacy with their boyfriends or girlfriends. Then they tell you they were in an empty house, watching a movie together with the lights out at 2:30 in the morning…and "somehow" they just went too far. HELLO?!

Create a plan for purity. Make choices ahead of time that will prepare and equip you for success.

3. *Rely on God's power.* This is the most important strategy in your war to remain pure.

God has given you all the strength you need to save yourself for marriage. As David said about the Lord in Psalm 16:8, "Because he is at my right hand, I will not be shaken." God will be your rock.

Relying on Him means that prayer is your most powerful weapon. Pray that the Lord will help you establish firm physical boundaries. Once you know your limits, pray earnestly that God will help you keep them. And pray immediately whenever you face a test of those limits.

Use God's power to develop your own resolve. Set your standards, and rely on His help to enforce them.

You can't depend on someone else to uphold your standards for you, but part of relying on God's power is to make sure you're accountable for your limits to someone besides your date. Write your boundaries down and show them to someone you trust. Share with him or her the progress of your war for purity. Allow that person to ask you the tough questions that will help keep you pure.

It's also helpful to share your boundaries with the person you're dating. In any dating relationship, make your boundaries clear early on. Ask your date to share his or her boundaries with you. After all, it's not just about you. You need to respect the other person's boundaries as well. You may think holding hands is fine, but if the other person doesn't, don't push it. Once you've discussed your personal limits, commit together to keep them.

Relying on God's power as the source for your own strength and resolve will make the difference in the war for purity. Stay close to your Savior, and you will succeed.

FIRST KISS

You may want me to tell you, in much more detail, exactly what's right for you when it comes to sexual boundaries. But in the end, *you* have to stand before God. That's why you must set your own boundaries according to His direction for your life.

I'll share part of my own story, however, and hope that it encourages you.

The first time I held hands with Jerusha, who's now my wife, I felt electricity and sparks. I knew then that anything more than the simplest of touches might cause me to stumble. And I knew that anything causing me to lust or stumble was "too far." So to keep my mind and body pure, I chose not to kiss her until the day we were engaged.

Believe me, there were times when this wasn't easy. But I'm sure I don't have to tell you how awesome our first kiss was. It was incredibly precious—because we'd waited. That kiss was totally worth the wait.

I'm not saying this has to be one of your boundaries too. I want you to build your own list of sexual standards—and to know exactly how and why you determined everything on that list. If the boundaries are truly your own, you'll be better able to follow them.

Stay confident, because you *can* successfully maintain sexual purity.

WHEN YOU'VE GONE TOO FAR

You may be feeling depressed right now because you've already crossed the boundary lines into what you know was inappropriate physical intimacy. Maybe you've even "gone all the way" and feel you can never get back to God's holiness. You're not alone. Most young people I surveyed felt that they had compromised their sexual purity at some point or another.

But no matter how far you have gone, you CAN turn back! *I promise!* You can change the course of your relationships, no matter how far astray they've gone.

I can tell you from experience that God can give you a new start. He can wipe the slate clean, and you will be pure in His eyes once again. There is hope for your hurting heart.

God's forgiveness isn't conditional; it isn't something that's applicable to some sins and not to others. He can cleanse you from ALL unrighteousness, including your sexual transgressions.

God's grace is so much greater than we can even imagine. He will always take you back! You can never fall beyond the reach of His loving, forgiving arms.

Author Madeleine L'Engle pictured it this way: "All of the sin that man could do, or even conceive of doing, is like one live coal tossed in the ocean of God's grace."

If you want to turn back to God, you can do it right now.

The first step in turning back to God is *confession*. The Lord assures us that "if we confess our sins, he is faithful and just and will forgive us our sins and purify us from all unrighteousness" (1 John 1:9).

The second step in turning back to God is to stop doing the sin. When Jesus forgave a woman guilty of adultery, He told her, "Go now and leave your life of sin" (John 8:11). Turning *to* God means turning *away* from your sinful ways. You must be willing to step away from all sexually immoral activity and live for purity instead.

The final step in turning back to God is *releasing your guilt.* God's Word says, "As far as the east is from the west, so far has he removed our transgressions from us" (Psalm 103:12). Your sin is gone! The Lord doesn't hold on to it, and neither should you.

With the confidence that you can never fall so far from God that He cannot bring you back, I hope you'll never again struggle with the question, "How far is too far?" I pray that you'll ask instead, "How pure can I be?"—and be filled with amazing joy as God shows you the answer.

Living in the Light

While I was working in the youth ministry at EV Free in Fullerton, the only things separating the church from my apartment building were Brea Boulevard and the parking lot of an abandoned shoe store. I lived in the apartment with Carl, another pastoral assistant, and we chose that humble abode because we could walk to work. If I had to be at the church at 8:30, guess when I left? 8:25 (or sometimes 8:29). It was sweet!

Our apartment was on the second floor, and our window faced the back of the shoe store, which had been deserted for several years. From this vantage point we could see everything that happened in the narrow alley behind the store.

The alley became an appliance graveyard with dead refrigerators popping up out of nowhere. People dumped other trash behind the store as well. With the piles of lumber and sheetrock left by local construction workers, Carl and I probably could have built a house.

The worst things happened at night. Because the building was vacant, no one paid the electric bill for the alley's floodlights. The darkness there led to all kinds of nighttime mischief. Cars would park in the shadows, and minutes later the windows would steam up. I don't have to give you three guesses to figure out what that means.

The place was nothing but bad news. In fact, one Wednesday night following the youth group's midweek Bible study, a pervert who had parked his van in the alley propositioned some of our students.

Naturally we were grateful when a dentist bought the old building. His construction crews remodeled everything, including the alley. They resurrected the floodlights, and those things shone baseball-stadium bright all night long. Darkness never fell on that alley again.

It was light that cleaned up the alley. No more midnight mischief, no more trash left to rot. In fact, from our second-story viewpoint, the alley actually looked pretty good.

I tell you this little story because it illustrates how light drives away darkness. Dark hides all kinds of things and makes sin and mischief easier. But light conquers the dark.

IN THE LIGHT

Think of the light behind the shoe store as God's presence. The force of it drove the sin in that alley away for good.

When God illuminates the dark places of your life, they can be cleansed just as that alley was. When you live in the light of God's presence, sin and shame will not overwhelm you.

In Psalm 89:15 we find this praise to God: "Blessed are those who have learned to acclaim you, who walk in the light of your presence, O LORD."

Your dating life *must* remain in the light of God. True freedom comes when nothing is hidden from God.

Just so you know, no matter how good you may be at hiding

things, you can never fool God. If your dating relationships are hidden, secretive, and "dark," God already knows. "He knows what lies in darkness" (Daniel 2:22). And not only does He know, He also cares. In every area of your life, He rejoices when you choose light instead of darkness.

WHY ARE WE SNEAKING AROUND?

Sneaking around, deception, and manipulation are not part of living in the light. Sadly, too many dating relationships (even among Christians) are full of secrets and lies.

When dating, you should never have to deceive or betray your parents, your friends, or your faith—never. No relationship justifies sneaking around. That kind of manipulation is sin. Don't try to downplay it. Sneaking around always causes pain and dissension among families and friends. Sneaking around also selfishly places your desires above the good of everyone else.

Make no mistakes; hidden sin is destructive. In Psalm 32, David reveals what living with a sin was like before he finally confessed it: "When I kept silent, my bones wasted away" (32:3). The agony of deception will eventually overwhelm you.

But Psalm 32 also teaches us the hope that comes with repentance and confession. David continues, "Then I acknowledged my sin to you and did not cover up my iniquity…and you forgave the guilt of my sin" (verse 5). God will forgive you when you stop covering up and sneaking around.

Maybe you're too young to date, but you've been sneaking around anyway. Stop.

Maybe you're dating someone your parents don't approve of, so you sneak around to see him or her. Stop.

Maybe your physical relationship has gotten out of control, and you lie and sneak to cover it up. Stop.

Sneaking around is always sinful!

And you can always stop it. Here's how.

First, take your sins to the Lord and ask for His forgiveness. If you confess your wrongdoing, He will forgive you.

The next step is a bit more difficult. It involves asking forgiveness from those whom you've deceived. After God's light cleanses you, you must then reconcile with others.

HELP FROM YOUR PARENTS

To shed His light in your life, God can use your parents as well as other faithful adults. In Proverbs we're instructed, "My son, keep your father's commands and do not forsake your mother's teaching.... For these commands are a lamp, this teaching is a light, and the corrections of discipline are the way to life" (6:20,23).

Listen to the guidance of parents and older believers. Be willing to give them an account of your actions. Don't get me wrong; you don't have to tape-record your conversations with your friends to play back to your parents. But you should be able to share everything without shame.

My former youth pastor, Ted Montoya, has three beautiful daughters. Though they are still too young to date, they've already discussed the matter thoroughly with their parents. Ted and his girls even wrote a family mission statement about dating. Each member of the family has agreed to the mission statement, and they regularly review it as a family.

The fundamental principle of the Montoya mission statement is that "no part is greater than the whole." That means none of the individual members are more important than the whole family. The good of their "whole" family supersedes all personal desires of the "parts."

When it comes to dating, the Montoyas have decided that it's in the family's best interest to maintain complete honesty. Ted prays that as his girls grow older, they'll keep their dating relationships accountable to the family.

To be accountable means being able to give an answer to another person for all your actions. Ted's family decided that everything that happens on a date should be open for discussion. His family has agreed not to hide and not to sneak.

Ted prays that when his girls are old enough to go out on dates, they'll remember that they must answer for each of their choices. He hopes they'll remember that the good of the whole overrules the desires of the parts.

The Montoyas chose to make these commitments because Ted has seen how dating without accountability can damage families. I've seen it too. I've witnessed families torn apart by one member who believed he or she was more important than the whole.

Just recently, a young woman in our youth group chose to place herself above her family and friends. She began dating a young man whom neither her parents nor her close Christian friends approved of. Her parents tried to guide and counsel her. They wanted to see their daughter in a Christian relationship. Instead, she chose a relationship that required her to lie and deceive.

She began to disrespect her family's rules and break curfews. When her parents grounded her for disobedience, she would sneak around anyway. Though caught in numerous lies, she refused to change her ways.

Now she has moved out of her parents' home and in with her

boyfriend. She's broken their hearts and stopped coming to church altogether. This young woman destroyed the peace and joy of her family because she thought her own desires were more significant than the good of her whole family. She decided that her relationship is more important than her family, her friends, and her faith. She placed the good of one "part" above the good of the "whole."

Help from Your Friends

This girl not only rebelled against her parents but also chose to disregard her Christian friends. On many occasions her friends tried to talk with her and advise her. Seeing the devastation she was causing, they wanted to help. If she had listened, they could have helped her recognize what she couldn't see on her own.

Part of the reason God has given us friends is to counteract our blindness to potential danger. We all have our blind spots, but God uses faithful friends to expand our limited perspective.

I can tell you from experience that the best friends are those who boldly speak up to help you see your blind spots. "The pleasantness of one's friend springs from his earnest counsel" (Proverbs 27:9). The best friends will offer serious counsel to "spur one another on toward love and good deeds" (Hebrews 10:24).

True friends speak the truth in love, even if you don't want to hear what they have to say. True friends keep you accountable.

Why We Need Help

Friendship accountability is the key to maintaining your emotional and physical boundaries. I agree with Chuck Swindoll's words in *Rise and Shine:* "I know of nothing more effective for maintaining a pure heart and keeping one's life balanced and on target than being part of an accountability group."

Earlier in the book, I recommended that you show your lists of emotional and physical boundaries to someone you trust. The reason is so your accountability partner can check up on you. We all need the help and encouragement of friends, especially when it comes to something that can be as confusing as dating.

Hebrews 3:12-13 gives us a great explanation of accountability along with the command to guard one another: "See to it, brothers, that none of you has a sinful, unbelieving heart that turns away from the living God. But encourage one another daily...so that none of you may be hardened by sin's deceitfulness." Sin will lead you astray, but friends can lead you back.

In *The Message,* Eugene Peterson translates the same passage this way: "So watch your step, friends. Make sure there's no evil unbelief lying around that will trip you up and throw you off course, diverting you from the living God.... Keep each other on your toes so sin doesn't slow down your reflexes."

Godly friendships will "keep you on your toes" and protect you from blindly falling into sin.

THE CREW

While I was at the Master's College, the Lord showed me how valuable true accountability can be. At school I met Brian Aaby, Darryl Goltiao, and Anthony Naimo, who to this day are my best friends.

The four of us quickly became close and hung out often.

Eventually we decided we wanted to keep one another accountable in our walks with Christ. All four of us agreed to be totally honest and to listen to one another's counsel.

Once a month "The Crew" would dine at the Hollywood Spaghetti Factory and catch up on the details of life. We confessed our sins to one another, prayed for one another, and made commitments to live holier lives. We followed up on those commitments because we desired to live in the light and because we knew we'd have to give account next time we met.

After two years of this, we graduated from college. Our surroundings changed, but the relationships didn't. We now live in four different states, but distance cannot destroy the strong bonds of friendship we've built. I continue to be accountable to Brian and Anthony in weekly phone calls, and I'm frequently in touch with Darryl as well.

These men of God have consistently called me on the carpet. To this day I trust and seek their wise counsel. Since 1993, not a month has gone by that I haven't talked with them. Now that's true friendship.

The Crew always encouraged one another to date on God's glory. We asked the hard questions and expected honest answers. Even after I decided to marry Jerusha, these men continued to be my number-one advisors. I don't know how I could have made it without their friendship and counsel.

When I told Anthony I wanted to propose to Jerusha, he insisted on coming out from Arizona to meet her. Because I trust Anthony implicitly, I would have listened if he was hesitant about our relationship. It meant a lot to me that he approved and that he recognized in Jerusha the same young woman of character that I saw. He even helped me plan the details of my proposal.

Before I got married, Brian also counseled me in a number of areas. We spent hours on the phone talking about the difficulties and joys of relationships. He gave me great advice from the two years of experience he had with his wife, Elisabeth.

GETTING REAL WITH ACCOUNTABILITY

It's not enough for me to tell you about accountability. It's not enough for you to simply show someone your list of boundaries. You must apply these truths to your dating life if you hope to see the benefits of accountability. So here are some steps you can take to make your dating life accountable:

Find someone. Your accountability partner should be someone you can trust with anything and everything, because you must be completely open and honest in order for accountability to work. Also, make sure to choose someone of the same sex. Talking about your dating struggles with a member of the opposite sex could lead to misunderstandings and false intimacy.

You can start with one accountability partner, or—what's even better—you can team up with two or more partners.

Be consistent. Set up a time and follow through. Whether it's once a month or twice a week, be consistent in your meeting times. If your accountability partner is starting to slack off, he or she may be hiding something.

Establish guidelines for your accountability times. Make these times separate from just hanging out. You may want to write a list of questions that the other person could ask you about your dating relationships. Discuss areas of weakness, such as thoughts, touching, and honesty.

Be willing to listen. Accountability works as long as you're committed to listening to each other and trusting each other's judgment. If your accountability partner thinks someone you're dating is leading you into sin, heed his or her advice. Believe that this person wants the best for you and for your walk with Christ.

P.S. God gave you two ears and one mouth! Use them accordingly. Don't let your own talk dominate the time.

Be willing to say the tough thing. A time may come when you need to confront your partner. When it does, "remember this: Whoever turns a sinner from the error of his way will save him from death and cover over a multitude of sins" (James 5:20). You can help someone avoid sin by speaking truthfully and boldly.

Speak the truth in love. This command is straight out of Ephesians 4:15. When you must confront your partner with sin, do so in a loving way. Dating is a tough issue because romantic feelings can be strong and deceptive. Speak the truth compassionately and you'll win respect and trust; speak harshly and you may push someone further away.

Be specific in your commitments. Set measurable goals. Don't just say, "I'm going to live a godly life this week." Commit that you'll avoid improper speech. Commit that you'll avoid inappropriate alone time with a guy or girl. Commit that you'll immediately confess any lustful thoughts, asking the Lord to renew your mind. Make real commitments.

Pray for one another. Pray for the commitments you've made and for specific needs and areas of weakness. Pray together and pray on your own. "Confess your sins to each other and pray for each other so that you may be healed. The prayer of a righteous man is powerful and effective" (James 5:16). Through prayer you can be part of God's healing and cleansing in each other's lives.

Above all, remember your position in Christ. You're a child of the light and have all the strength and power of the living God to help you uphold your commitments. "For you were once darkness, but now you are light in the Lord. Live as children of light (for the fruit of the light consists in all goodness, righteousness and truth) and find out what pleases the Lord. Have nothing to do with the fruitless deeds of darkness, but rather expose them" (Ephesians 5:8-11).

Just for Girls, Just for Guys

A Closer Focus

Now for something different.

This chapter is filled with advice specifically tailored either just for guys or just for girls (and I'm grateful to Jerusha for special help on the girls' parts).

From the headings in the text, you'll be able to quickly tell which sections are for you—or maybe you'll want to just go ahead and read everything. (It can't hurt.)

If You're a Guy: Stay Out of the Jungle

During my years at the Master's College, I lived in Waldock, which to this day is still the best guys' dorm there. Waldock housed around eighty rowdy male students. As you can imagine, living there was a blast.

Truly a "guys" dorm, Waldock hosted a series of battles known as the Praying Mantis War. We had caught a praying mantis and were curious about what other creatures he would fight (and eat). After we watched him conquer other insects, it was time for the Praying Mantis versus Black Widow Showdown, in which our prized mantis ripped the spider to shreds.

Yes, the testosterone ran thick at Waldock.

With eighty men living in such close proximity, we all became pretty close. We would talk about (what else?) guys' issues—sports, practical jokes, and dating. Truthfully, girls and dating made up most of our conversations.

When any one of us started spending time with a certain girl, the rest of us knew it immediately, becoming curious and sometimes even suspicious. We'd watch him walk a girl to the cafeteria or hang with her for hours in the lounge. If the pattern continued, one of us would eventually ask, "So, are you two a thing or what?"

Everyone would hover around to hear the response. If his answer came back, "Yeah, we're dating," he was in for merciless teasing (all in good fun).

But if he responded, "No," we'd get concerned. Sometimes, of course, a guy would say no because nothing had been set in stone. We also knew, however, that some guys will lead girls "into the jungle," a phrase the Waldock boys coined after hearing a sermon about responsible dating and relationships.

Leading a girl into the jungle meant leading her on with no intentions to follow through in a relationship. After a while the guy abandons her, leaving her helpless and confused—in the jungle.

Those of us who wanted to protect the ladies on campus didn't tolerate guys who took the jungle route. It just wasn't right. He'd be confronted by someone (usually a friend) and asked if he was being honest about his intentions. We didn't want to bully anyone; we just wanted each man to realize his responsibility to the young women with whom he spent time.

Nine times out of ten, the guy would respond well. Either he'd wake up and see what the rest of us saw—that it looked like they were a couple—or he'd admit that he'd been wrong from the beginning. For the most part, the guys at Master's were responsible gentlemen. They didn't want to hurt their lady friends.

This jungle tale has a point: You need to be aware of how your actions affect young women. I've seen too many girls led into the jungle by guys who had no intention of leading them out.

"He who leads the upright along an evil path will fall into his own trap, but the blameless will receive a good inheritance" (Proverbs 28:10). If you lead a Christian girl into the jungle, you may be trapped by that sin. On the other hand, if you conduct your relationships without shame, your reward will be great.

It's worth it to have pure motives and clear intentions. It's worth it to stay out of the jungle.

Of course I know that many young women are also guilty of stringing their dates along. I don't claim that guys are the only culprits. However, I address this to you as a man because I believe firmly in your responsibility to learn to lead, particularly in relationships.

More on that later…Let's first offer the women some stage time.

IF YOU'RE A GIRL: HOW TO BAIT THE HOOK

If you've ever fished before (don't worry, I won't go too far with this), you know that certain baits attract certain types of fish. If you want to catch trout, you wouldn't use shark bait.

The same principle applies to attracting young men. The type of bait you use determines the fish you'll catch. A tattooed, body-pierced, leather-wearing woman may not grab my attention, but she certainly might attract a hard-core Harley-Davidson type.

Let me ask you this: Would you want someone to be attracted to you simply because he saw the outline of your bra through your blouse or because your legs looked nice in a short skirt?

I hope you answered with a resounding no! If you desire to attract respectable men, you must strive to be a respectable woman. The way you dress has a lot to do with this.

Think of your clothing as a table of contents. No author would give away the whole book in the table of contents. Don't mess with revealing that much of yourself. Instead, bait your hook with purity and respect, and you'll attract a fish you won't have to throw back!

Later we'll discuss more about modesty in how you dress. For now I want to address another aspect of "baiting the hook." Let's discuss flirting.

Let me assure you that I know young men struggle with this issue just as much as girls do. I bring this issue to you, a woman, because I believe you can take a stand to stop flirting. You can do it in two ways: One, stop initiating flirtatious conversation and touching, and two, stop responding to the same.

To flirt means to act amorously or court playfully *without serious intentions.* When you flirt, you string along and toy.

So what's wrong with that?

Playful flirtation is deceptive (and therefore wrong) because it pretends that feelings exist when they don't. Flirting also manipulates someone into liking a false "you."

Here are some other reasons why flirting should be avoided:

- Flirting seeks attention in improper ways.
- Even when done in fun, flirting often ends with one person or the other developing strong feelings. When that person is later

rejected, he may be heartbroken and disappointed. Your flirtation has caused another's pain, in violation of the second greatest commandment to "love your neighbor as yourself."
- Others may get the wrong impression about you and expect you to follow through on your playful promises.
- Flirting tends to attract the wrong kinds of guy friends while alienating your friends who are girls.

This last point deserves special attention. A woman who constantly flirts rarely has strong friendships with other girls. They react to a flirt with either jealously or hatred.

Flirtatious girls tend to develop many guy friendships, and often do so quickly. These friendships don't last, however, because they're based on games. If the guy wants more and she disappoints, he usually won't stick around just to "save the friendship."

Flirting wields real power. Even the Bible notes how easily a man can fall for a coy woman. In the Song of Songs a man says to his beloved, "You have stolen my heart with one glance of your eyes" (4:9). That was just one look. Imagine what damage long-term flirtatious conversation and playful touching can do.

You also need to know how much your touch can affect us guys. When you put your hand on ours or brush against us, it's intense. Please recognize that your touch is powerful.

Hugging can also present problems. I'm all for hugs, but please don't press your bodies against ours. Side hugs are usually safer between guys and girls. If you do hug face to face, think about putting some space between you and the man. You can either put your hand out to protect your chest, or you can stand far enough away to make it a light hug.

I know this seems like a lot to consider, and in some ways it is. The more you think about your actions and how they affect others, however, the more able you'll be to honor your Lord, yourself, and your brothers in Christ.

Stay tuned for a look at modesty…

IF YOU'RE A GUY: WHAT GOD INTENDS

Today's society has terribly skewed the idea of biblical masculinity and leadership. Feminism rants against stereotypical male tyrants who rule their homes and families with the iron fist of so-called male leadership. By these accounts, biblical masculinity appears ugly and undesirable.

Society also claims that leadership has nothing to do with gender. Because of this, many confused men have shied away from leadership responsibilities. Women have been forced to counterbalance.

As a result, our society breeds passive men who lack vision and direction and overaggressive women who attempt to protect and provide for themselves. God never intended men and women to function this way.

We cannot look to the world to define masculinity and male leadership for us. We must look to what God says about it. God created men to lead. He created men to be accountable. He created men to protect.

In the opening pages of Genesis, the Lord creates Adam as ruler of the earth. When He creates Eve, she shares in the charge as Adam's helper and completer; Adam remains God's appointed leader.

Adam's leadership results from his position in creation. God's original plan included an order. He could have decided Eve would come first, but He didn't. Male leadership is not a result of the Fall or the Curse. God always intended men to lead.

God also intended men to be accountable. The Lord holds Adam responsible for eating the forbidden fruit. Try as he may to blame Eve, the buck stops with him.

God had set Adam over Eve to protect her. He was to guard her as his life-mate. Adam failed to protect Eve in her encounter with the serpent, and, as we see in Genesis 3, Adam had to answer for this failure to lead and protect.

In the Creation account, God sets a pattern for masculine-feminine relationships. The man bears the weight of responsibility and leadership. We witness this truth throughout the pages of Scripture. God elects men to be kings, priests, apostles, and elders, and these masculine leaders must give to the Lord an account of their leadership.

And what does that leadership mean?

We'll look at that next when I come back to you…

IF YOU'RE A GIRL: MODESTY IS SOMETHING YOU ARE

In the youth ministries I've worked with, the staff members have consistently encouraged the young women of the group to dress and behave modestly and above reproach. We've still faced problems though.

For example, the youth room at EV Free in Fullerton was an amphitheater. Large carpeted steps tiered upward from a ground-level stage. The students would sit on the steps instead of chairs so everyone could see the stage.

This configuration made sitting modestly a necessity. Sitting on the steps, young women couldn't simply cross their legs as they could in a chair. Unfortunately, many young ladies were not as conscious of their skirts and dresses as they should have been.

As shorter skirts came into style, it seemed impossible for some young women to sit modestly in the amphitheater. Even if they tried, either there wasn't enough fabric on their short skirts or they had never been taught to sit appropriately.

The other pastoral assistants and I were troubled by the problem. We made a point to approach the subject through our female leaders, but the modesty issues didn't disappear. In fact, every summer we would face a whole slew of modesty dilemmas.

Since our church was located about thirty minutes from the beach, we would take a busload of students there once a week. We instituted a one-piece bathing suit rule, which we hoped would eliminate some of the modesty issues. Instead, it created a myriad of problems.

Although some of the ladies chose classy and modest one-pieces, many wore suits that, though one-piece, seemed more immodest than some bikinis.

The troubles got worse. Some of the more rebellious students would actually drive down to the beach separately and flaunt their two-piece-suit freedom.

Some people might say that the young men of our group could have treated those girls modestly by turning away. These same people would claim that modesty is something you "give" a person.

I disagree with this opinion. Modesty is not something others give you; it's something you *are*. Modesty is a state of being; it involves how you think and act. Modesty affects every part of your life, from speech to dress to how you sit.

You don't have to wear a string bikini to be immodest. You can be immodest in a knee-length skirt if you aren't aware of how you sit, stand, and walk. You can be immodest in a long-sleeve blouse if your buttonholes gape or you bend over too far.

A lot of young women don't want to think about details like

these. They want freedom to wear what they like. They want to believe that their choices don't affect others. Fashion and peer pressures perpetuate this lie.

God sends quite a different message. In 1 Timothy 2:9, He states, "I also want women to dress modestly, with decency and propriety." In this verse, *modest* means respectable, worthy, kind, appropriate, suitable, righteous, and just. Are these not virtues every young lady should cultivate?

Modest also means unobtrusive, or not getting in someone's way. Imagine how troublesome a woman's improper dress and behavior can be to a young man's purity. And when a girl sports the latest fashions without thinking, imagine what a stumbling block it can be for her sisters in Christ who may be trying to honor God with their dress, but who feel a pressure from her to dress immodestly.

IF YOU'RE A GUY: BE A MAN

In his book *Tender Warrior: God's Intention for a Man,* Stu Weber explains, "To be masculine is to take initiative. To provide direction, security, and order.... It means taking the lead."

God created men to initiate and women to respond to their leadership. Weber likens the man's role to that of a trail scout who surveys the course ahead, determines the direction, and sets the pace.

Please understand: God created men and women as equals. God created both men and women in His image. Men and women are equal in their humanity and in their dignity. Both receive the free gift of grace in Christ Jesus, and both share eternal life with Him.

God also created men and women with different purposes. Their roles in creation have nothing to do with equality or superiority. Their roles are merely reflections of God's purpose and order.

Like it or not, God chose you, a guy, as a leader. You've been appointed for leadership, and it's a great honor. God wants you to grow in servant leadership, becoming more like Christ with each step.

But beware—many men abuse this gift of leadership. To lead isn't about being macho or having power. True leadership is about service. If we're to lead well, we will follow the example of Christ. We'll put others first, not try to control them.

Your choice to lead, to protect, and to be accountable starts now. Your dating relationships can be excellent preparation for a lifetime of servant leadership. Use this time wisely.

Learn to apply the truths of masculinity and practice servant leadership in your dating life. God longs for men who will lead with love, direction, vision, and purpose. You can start to become that kind of man in your dating experiences.

As the initiator, you can direct your dates either to God's glory or to your own pleasures. As the protector, you can uphold a young woman's purity or compromise God's standards. Whichever road you choose, you will have to answer to God.

As a male created by God, you must learn to lead, to be accountable, and to protect. Then you will begin to understand true masculinity.

Simply being male does not make you a man. It's easy to be just "male" and to shrug off the responsibilities and privileges of being a man. But God doesn't want a bunch of males; He wants men.

God wants men who will face up to the high call of leadership. He wants men who recognize they were appointed for responsibility. He wants masculine men who will take the lead in protecting and providing.

Pursue masculinity as God has ordained it. Read all that you can on becoming a godly man. Observe men of faith and family. Ask for advice and guidance from older men who've walked the path ahead of you. I challenge you, as a young male, to become a man.

IF YOU'RE A GIRL: A PRACTICAL GUIDE FOR HOW TO DRESS

Growing up, I remember watching my mom. She made modesty a high priority in our home. She always dressed appropriately and behaved properly. She honored her husband and her God with her appearance. My mom is a beautiful woman who modeled modesty for others.

You may not have a shining example of modesty at home as I did. And you may see the worst examples of immodesty every day at school. It's possible that you also spend time looking at fashion magazines, which are among the worst proponents of immodesty. But you *can* take responsibility to dress and behave modestly.

Being married, I now know a lot more about women's clothing. I've received a whole new education in women's apparel from my wife. Some of the following things I've learned can help you dress to glorify God and protect your purity:

- When bending over in a loose-fitting or scoop-neck blouse, always place your hand over the neckline.
- When wearing a button-down blouse, stand sideways and look at the buttonholes in a mirror. If they spread too far apart or gape too much, you'll expose your chest. Pin between the buttons if you need to.
- For all blouses, be conscious about your bra showing. Be especially careful with the armholes or straps of sleeveless

blouses. Just the sight of your undergarments can cause a guy to stumble.

- When wearing a dress or skirt, always stand in the light and check if you need a slip. Even a lightweight black dress can reveal your silhouette (in other words, be see-through). Your best bet is to always wear a slip. And if you can't find a slip short enough for your skirt, chances are your skirt is too short!
- When wearing a skirt or dress, always be conscious of the way you're sitting. You may think I don't need to mention this obvious fact, but you'd be surprised how often girls fail to sit modestly.
- When wearing a skirt, be aware that changing positions will cause your skirt to bunch or pull. Smooth your skirt down when you sit down or stand up.
- When choosing a bra, remember that lace and seams will show through many tops. Choose a seamless or smooth bra whenever possible. (And remember, it's almost pointless to wear a bra if the material of your blouse is too thin. I don't have to tell you what happens when you get cold. Protect yourself with a thicker material.)
- The best advice I could give you is to stand in front of a mirror before you go out. Bend over, turn side to side, turn around, and check everything. Be aware of what different kinds of clothing can reveal.

Don't leave your heart out of the check. Ask yourself why you're wearing what you're wearing. If you check your heart and find your motives are bad, you may want to change.

I'm confident that you desire to be pure in both dress and behavior. Modesty is not boring or burdensome. Modesty always honors and uplifts not only the person who displays it, but all those around her. So take great care to be modest.

GUY QUESTIONS

Q. How serious should I be about each dating relationship?

A. Very serious. You need to act with wisdom and responsibility in each relationship you start with a young woman.

God commands us to consider others more important than ourselves (Philippians 2:3). The more seriously you take your relationships, the less likely you'll be to carelessly hurt others.

The key is to proceed with caution. Consider her feelings and emotions. Really think before you speak and look before you leap! "The wisdom of the prudent is to give thought to their ways, but the folly of fools is deception" (Proverbs 14:8). Make this a banner verse for your dating life. As you give thought to your ways, you'll treat your date better every time. On the other hand, if you deceive her, you're sure to be the greatest of fools.

But let me clarify my first answer. If your question centers on whether every dating relationship should head toward serious commitment, the answer is no. I've emphasized in this book a more light-hearted approach to dating. I genuinely believe you can have fun, God-honoring dates without the question mark of a serious relationship hovering in the background.

My answer about being serious has more to do with your respect for her than the intensity of your relationship. Be serious about your personal commitment to honor her, but be easygoing and cautious about the development of your relationship.

As you grow older, your relationships will naturally be more intense because of your season of life. When is the right time to really get serious? I believe that through your prayer, your counsel from others, and your mutual determination, God will reveal the right timing for taking that step.

Q. How should I treat a girlfriend?

A. Treat her like a lady. Unfortunately it's not our second nature to treat a girl well. We have to learn how to honor young women.

A family in our church operates on the following standard: No young man should date until he learns to treat his mother and sisters as ladies. If that standard were universal, I doubt if half the guys out there would ever start dating. But at least some young men would know how to treat a lady right.

So how exactly do you treat a young woman as a lady? How do you treat someone as a sister in Christ?

You can start on your knees. No, I don't mean asking her forgiveness for all the times you've been a bonehead. I mean praying for her. Pray for God to bless her with wisdom, purity, and grace. Pray for her goals, dreams, and hopes. Pray for her relationships (particularly the one with you).

Ask her what she would have you pray for her. Let her know you're praying; that will definitely encourage her.

You can also encourage her with compliments and notes of affirmation. If you think she looks nice, tell her. If she said something especially kind, thank her for it. If she's down, write her to let her know you're thinking of her. You'll be blown away by how much these small things will lift her up.

Treating a girlfriend well also means respecting her. You demonstrate respect by listening to her and remembering the things she's told you. You show respect by opening the door for her and letting her go first in line. You prove your respect by speaking well of her whether she's around or not.

Many times a guy treats his girlfriend differently when his buddies are around—for some reason he thinks he has to become funny or tough or distant. But a gentleman treats his lady the same in all circumstances. Don't diss your friends, but be sure to pay attention to your girlfriend.

One last thing: Do activities that she enjoys doing. Sacrificing your own interests for the sake of hers really honors a woman. And I don't mean doing it but complaining the whole time. You honor her if you *graciously* do what she likes.

I could go on and on about how to treat a young lady; there's so much to learn. It's definitely a lifelong process to apply it all. I'm still learning, and I've never met a man who has it all down. The important thing is to continue growing and acting on the things we know.

GIRL QUESTIONS

Q. Should a girl ask a guy out?

A. This is one of the toughest questions for me to answer, and there are many conflicting opinions on the subject. Some people claim it's never appropriate for a young woman to initiate a date or even a conversation with a man. Others think girls should be free to ask anyone, anytime.

I fall somewhere in the middle on the opinion spectrum.

I believe there can be times when it's appropriate for a young lady to ask a guy out. On the other hand, I believe God designed an orderly and perfect way for men and women to interact in their relationships, and that in this design He created the man to lead, protect, and provide, and the woman to respond, nurture, and complete.

In Genesis 2, the Lord reveals that Adam is incomplete without Eve. Clearly different from man in physical makeup, woman also differed from man in purpose. Her purpose was to help and complete her husband. Adam was her protector, provider, and leader.

This pattern of male leadership and feminine response repeats itself throughout Scripture. Even the great metaphor of Christ and the church pictures a feminine bride (the church) responding to the servant-leadership of her masculine bridegroom (Christ).

This truth should be both liberating and exhilarating for you as a young woman. Your desire to nurture, create, and respond to life with strong emotions are God-given gifts. They are part of your very nature.

You have the unique privilege of portraying the church, the radiant bride of Christ, as you learn to respond to the leadership of godly men in your life. Your femininity is intricately tied to your responsiveness and help.

When it comes to marriage, the Lord clearly commands the man to lead and protect his family. He is the initiator and head. When it comes to dating, I believe the young man should take the lead as well.

I believe any young man you date should honor you as the feminine beauty God created you to be. He should protect your purity and your heart. He should provide a safe and fun environment for you. He should lead with godly service.

I leave it to you to decide whether he should lead in asking as well. I leave it to you because I believe your motive is what counts. Proverbs 16:2 tells us that "motives are weighed by the LORD."

Your motives for asking a young man out may be pure. You may simply want to enjoy being with a friend; you may just want to hang out and get to know someone better.

On the other hand, if you're motivated simply by a longing to have "someone," you might be asking for the wrong reasons. Look at your heart, and ask God to reveal your motives.

My wife, Jerusha, believes young women should focus on responding, not on asking. She compares this issue to dancing.

Jerusha loves to dance. She especially loves to partner dance, whether it be swing or ballroom or two-step. Partner dancing was created with a specific orderliness. The man "leads" the dance, and the woman "follows." If both dance their part, no toes are smashed or eyes poked out.

My wife learned to dance early in life and danced any occasion she could. Most of her dates, however, didn't know how to dance the steps, let alone lead. Jerusha taught them to dance by leading them through the steps.

My wife readily admits that learning to lead caused her a host of problems in dancing. When she actually wanted to follow a strong male lead, she had a difficult time because she had become so accustomed to directing herself. She had learned to lead but not to follow.

She feels she also learned to "lead" in dating relationships. She expressed strong opinions and ideas, and her dates tended to follow instead of initiate. Now she wishes she had learned to respond better.

I'm not going to tell you whether you should ever ask a guy out or not. In some instances it seems perfectly fine. But I'll emphasize to you that learning to respond is of utmost importance. At least then no toes will be smashed or eyes poked out!

Q. Why do I never get asked out?

A. So many young women I surveyed asked this or similar questions. Some masked their curiosity behind questions like, "How come guys always go for the same girls?" or "Why does it seem like looks are number one?" To all these questions, I want to offer the same answer:

You don't *need* a guy!

Please don't misinterpret me. I'm not male-bashing or telling you that all guys are jerks. Guys can be great friends and dates. Relationships can be fun and exciting. But you don't need a guy to validate who you are or make you feel special. You don't need a guy to make you worthy or important. You don't have to go to your senior prom to have a fulfilling life.

I know that sometimes it feels like life would be better if you got asked to the prom. Even the movies would be fine. But I promise you, life wouldn't improve that much.

Sure, you'd have fun for the night, but then you would worry about whether you had broccoli in your teeth after dinner, or if you smelled bad during the slow dancing because you were still sweating from the fast dancing. Worrying about dates doesn't end when you get asked out.

In my years of youth ministry, I've noticed that girls tend to fall into one of four categories. The first type sits at home, lamenting that she never gets asked out and crying every time she watches the *90210* prom special. She pines away for a boyfriend or for just one date. She desperately craves attention. And if she ever gets a date, she does almost anything to keep the guy.

The second type of girl bounces from guy to guy, dating everyone in sight. She's the queen of two-week relationships and the biggest flirt around. She has all kinds of guy friends but pushes away all the girls. She's too busy for girlfriends anyway. She has to be the center of attention or else she doesn't feel worthwhile. Deep down she fears that someday she will lose her appeal and no one will want her anymore.

The third type of girl dates only one guy at a time. She develops longer relationships, but "falls in love" every six months. She breaks off one serious relationship and immediately starts another. She can't stand to be alone. She likes the constant affirmations of love and value she gets from a boyfriend. She can't imagine herself without someone.

The fourth type of girl finds her identity in Christ and knows that she's worth more than anything a guy could offer. She recognizes that her friendships with both girls and guys are strongest when she loves others as Christ loves her, without expectation. She develops deep relationships because she doesn't need attention from others; she's secure in the love and attention she receives from the Lord. She wants companionship from others, not adoration. She doesn't need dates, though she welcomes them if they come. She knows that whether she dates or not, she is worthy and complete.

I hope you want to be like the fourth young woman I described—secure, strong, and able to have true and meaningful relationships with others.

I'll repeat: You don't need a guy!

MORE GUY QUESTIONS

Q. How do I take leadership in a bad situation?

A. Let's clarify what a bad situation is. Imagine that you and your girlfriend have been dating for a few months. You decide to rent a movie one night and go back to your parents' house. When you get there, you find out everyone has gone out for the evening. You think you'll be okay on your own, but about an hour later the two of you are struggling to maintain your physical boundaries. What do you do?

Even if you've set good physical boundaries, you may find yourself in potentially compromising situations. Don't be discouraged or surprised by that. The Enemy loves to attack you in places you think you're strong. Instead of allowing him to catch you off guard, you should have a plan for these possibly explosive circumstances.

As the man, you need to lead your date out of the danger zone. This could be pretty humbling, because you'll have to admit that you've let things get out of control.

First, stop whatever you were doing. If you had the lights off and a movie on, flip those light switches on and turn the movie off. That simple step will break some of the tension.

Depending on the severity of the situation, you should either direct your date to another activity or just take her home.

Use wisdom. If you lead her back into the danger zone, next time it will be harder to get out. Sometimes it's best to just call it a night and end on a good note.

As soon as you can, tell her that you were wrong. Accept responsibility for your part and don't make excuses. Let go of your pride and say you're sorry.

Voice your concern. It may be hard to do, but talk to her about what you felt uncomfortable with. (You need to actually say the words.) If you feel any twinge of doubt about what you're doing with your date, you probably shouldn't be doing it.

Q. What things should I avoid in a relationship?

A. The top five things I wish young adults would avoid in dating relationships are obsession, jealous rages, fear, the love-hate cycle, and out-of-control physicality.

Obsessive relationships are characterized by spending too much time together, the inability or lack of desire to think of anything else, and "checking out" of the rest of life. If you realize that you've lost all your friends, ignored your family for months, and found yourself writing her name over and over instead of writing your science report, you may want to consider whether you've become obsessed. You should always feel that you can let go of the relationship and still have a life of your own.

You should also avoid jealous rages. Jealousy seems to be a rampant problem among young adults. Stormy displays of jealousy and even violence are becoming more common. Most often, jealousy arises out of insecurity and lack of trust. If you're prone to jealousy, check your temper and your words. Don't blow up over petty issues.

Fear goes hand in hand with jealousy. Both spring from insecurity and both will eat away at you. If you constantly worry about being rejected, cheated on, or broken up with, you may want to reevaluate whether you're ready for a relationship. Relationships must be built on trust. If you simply can't trust someone yet, back off for a while. Let the Lord teach you about faithfulness outside the dating circle. Then you can reenter when you feel less anxious.

Avoid the love-hate roller coaster. If you break up, then get back together only to break up all over again, you're heading nowhere. Look for and follow the signs in your relationship. An on-again off-again relationship causes a lot of stress and confusion. It's better to be friends consistently than to be dating in a love-hate cycle.

Last, but certainly not least, please don't let the physical side of your relationship spiral out of control. From what I've seen, lack of accountability in a physical relationship damages young people more than any other dating problem. You must keep your physical relationship aboveboard. Don't be afraid to ask for advice and help. You can and will see the benefits of asking for wisdom from others who have traveled the road a bit longer.

MORE GIRL QUESTIONS

Q. What's the best way to turn someone down?

A. Since girls tend to get asked out more than guys do, it's the girls who most often have to answer yes or no. So what happens when you want to say no?

Some girls don't have a problem with this. They laugh in the guy's face and say, "As if!" Hopefully you aren't quite that tactless.

What if you truly don't want to hurt someone's feelings, but you just don't want to go out with him? What if you can't see yourself developing a closer relationship and don't want to lead him on?

Just be honest. You don't have to have an excuse (like the old "I've got to wash my hair" line). You don't even need a reason. "No" is reason enough.

I know it may sound hard to be honest, but it's a lot easier than breaking things off after the guy has bought you a ring or something.

If a guy knows right away that you aren't interested, the ball's in his court. He can always opt to put himself on the chopping block by asking you out again. If he does choose to do that, at least it's his problem and not yours. Most guys won't endure this humiliation though. They will suck it up and move on.

When you say yes because you don't want to hurt his feelings, you end up hurting him more than if you'd been honest in the first place. Once a girl says yes to a guy, his hopes and anticipations for the relationship double. Don't put him through the pain of delayed disappointment.

Remember, being honest doesn't translate into being rude or

obnoxious. Say no sensitively. There are many ways to graciously phrase a negative response. Come up with some ways to say no honestly yet sensitively. That way, when the situation arises, you won't be searching for words.

Being honest also doesn't translate into making an excuse. Don't say, "Oh, I'm already busy for Friday." If you say that, he may well ask you out the next Friday and the next. If you're busy every Friday, he may start with Saturdays.

If you tell him you'll "think about it," but never plan to accept, you've just lied. You never meant to think about it; you just wanted to get out of the situation as quickly as possible.

Just say no if you don't want to go out. Don't worry about whether he'll tell other people you're a jerk. If you were sensitive and honest, you know his accusations are unfounded. Act on your convictions, and you'll find that saying no isn't as tough as it may seem.

Q. When it comes to physical issues, how do I say no effectively?

A. When someone pushes your physical boundaries, they declare war on your purity. You have every right to defend yourself and uphold your standards. You should never have to feel afraid to speak up and say no.

When you do need to enforce your boundaries, be firm and be vocal. The more emphatically you say no, the clearer your message will be. If you playfully say, "Hey, c'mon," or softly whisper, "Don't do that, please," you're being too weak. You need to be firm. Say no loudly enough for him to be startled. Hopefully that kind of response will cause him to rethink what he's doing and change his course.

Also, don't assume that simply pushing his hand away will solve things. You need to verbalize that his behavior is unacceptable. Tell him no. Body language alone won't cut it. You have to make it obvious, blunt, and clearer than day.

If you follow the guidelines in this book for developing good physical boundaries, you may encounter someone pushing your limits to see if you mean business. Don't stand for it!

If you've said no once and the trouble continues, get out of the situation. Ask him to take you home. If he won't, call a family member or a close friend to pick you up. Get out of the heat of the moment any way you can.

Don't be worried about what he'll think, what he'll tell other people, or whether he'll ask you out again. Worry instead that he doesn't respect you enough to uphold your boundaries! Any guy who crosses your borders isn't worth a teaspoon of your spit. (That's gross, but I'm serious.)

From personal experience, I can tell you that nothing means more to a husband than knowing that his wife upheld her physical boundaries. That's a woman he can respect, cherish, and trust. Be that kind of pure bride for your husband. Say no *firmly* and *vocally*, then get out of the situation.

As you pursue godly femininity, know that the Lord is honored. I'm thankful for this chance to encourage you to be a woman of character.

ONE FINAL GUYS' ISSUE

Before I close this marathon chapter, I want to cover one other area specific to you as a man. I don't want to pull any punches here. Let's talk about pornography.

Most guys I know and most male students I've counseled have struggled with pornography in one form or another. With the availability of pornography in magazines, movies, and on the radio and Internet, it's easier than ever to get away with indulging the lusts of the flesh.

In a magazine for pastors, I recently saw pornography defined as "all sexually oriented material intended primarily to arouse the reader, viewer, or listener."

Pornography isn't limited to *Playboy* magazine and X-rated movies. Pornographic material can show up in a note from someone at school, on your morning radio show, in TV commercials, or on a Web site you heard about from a friend. If it aims at arousing you sexually, it's pornography.

You may not think this is a big deal. You may think you're okay watching those Cinemax specials with "some nudity," or hanging a scantily clad poster girl on your closet door. But pornography is more serious than you can imagine. It is a beast that will slowly devour and enslave you.

In another magazine article, the author asks, "Is it really possible that viewing hundreds of perfect-looking naked women has no effect on the way a man sees his wife, or girlfriend, or women in general?" The answer is no. An emphatic and deadly serious NO!

Pornography is a lie that corrodes God's truth about sex and love. Pornography promises but cannot deliver. It entices and allures but it never fulfills.

Instead of looking at women as objects of God's beauty and glory, pornography teaches you to look at women as objects of your fantasy and pleasure. It lies to you about who women are and should be.

I promise you, if you allow pornography any place in your mind, you won't be able to handle yourself in relationships with the opposite sex. At school, parties, the beach, the pool, or even at church, you'll begin to undress women with your eyes. You'll start seeing them as the objects of your desire and lust rather than the partners in glory God created them to be.

Pornography is devastating and ruthless, but it can be overcome. Here are a few strategies for success in the spiritual battle against pornography:

- *Recognize the battle.* Pornography is a spiritual battle for your mind. The battle begins when you allow sexual thoughts or fantasies to go unchecked. Then you must wage war against the temptation to dwell on and indulge in those desires. Pornography is a lethal drug, and the battle is for our minds and bodies.

- *Never assume you're "above it."* In *Point Man,* Steve Farrar writes, "We can never deceive ourselves into thinking we are somehow above sexual sin. The moment you begin to view yourself in that light, you can be sure that your carcass will one day be hanging in cold storage." Enough said.

- *Pray.* You can win the battle against lust and pornography only by relying on God's strength and guidance. "You are safe," writes Chuck Swindoll in *Come Before Winter,* "just as long as you draw upon your Savior's strength. Try to handle it yourself and you'll lose—every time." You *must* pray for God's help in each and every situation.

- *Flee.* As I mentioned in the chapter on sexual boundaries, God wants you to flee sexual temptation. He doesn't want you to stand there and take it or try to fight on your own. He wants you to get out of there, and quick. If you struggle with cable channels or magazines, ask your dad to cancel the subscriptions. Ask your mom to throw away the Victoria's Secret catalogue. Ask your carpool driver if he or she would mind listening to music instead of talk radio. If you struggle with the Internet, never use it unless you're with other people who can keep you accountable.

- *Take captive every thought.* In 2 Corinthians 10:5 we're commanded to "demolish…every pretension that sets itself up against the knowledge of God, and…take captive every thought to make it obedient to Christ." Imagine capturing your ugly thought, tying it up with ropes and chains, and marching it straight to Jesus. Create a mental picture of gaining victory over that thought. Do this with *every single thought* that threatens to distract you with inappropriate sexual desire.
- *Be accountable.* Don't overlook this powerful weapon in the war on pornography. Confess your trouble spots to another man, and be accountable to him. If you consistently have someone asking you about your thought life and actions, you'll be more likely to live purely. Most likely the man you ask will want your help in return. Stay accountable in every area.

I know you may face a fierce struggle in this area. It may be an on-again off-again thing or a constant, day-to-day battle. Whatever the case, there is hope…and there is redemption. God can free you if you're willing to call on Him for help.

Inquiring Minds Want to Know

MORE QUESTIONS...AND ANSWERS

When I was growing up, a tabloid newspaper called the *National Enquirer* used to run ads on television. The paper's slogan was "Inquiring Minds Want to Know...I Want to Know."

We used to laugh at the ads because the newspaper was so ridiculous. The *Enquirer* headlined stories like "Man Delivers Seven-Pound Baby" and "Elvis Spotted on Mount Everest." People who believed that junk can't have much rolling around upstairs.

The *Enquirer* claimed that they continued publishing such stories because that's what the public wanted to know about. Readers kept requesting information on fantastical stories like extraterrestrial aliens or the Loch Ness monster.

When I surveyed several youth groups, I asked students to tell me what they most wanted to know about dating. Luckily I didn't get too many weird requests. No one wanted to know if guys could get pregnant or if Elvis was available. I did get some pretty good questions though.

In the previous chapter, I addressed some of the specific "guy" and "girl" queries. In this final chapter, we'll deal with the questions and answers that affect both guys and girls—the top issues on their inquiring minds.

YOU WANT TO KNOW

Q. Where should we go on dates?

A. Sky's the limit! This isn't a book on creative dating, but there are some easy ways to spice up your dates and get beyond the movie theater.

Most dates include some kind of meal, so why not be creative in your choice of restaurants? So many cuisines to try, so little time. Have you ever tried Thai, Ethiopian, Indian, or Moroccan? If you like chow mein, chances are you'll love Pad Thai, a noodle dish with meat and vegetables. If you're worried about flipping something onto your date with your fork, go for Ethiopian, where you use a delicious spongy type of bread to eat all your dishes. Moroccan and Indian will wow your senses with tantalizing spices and scents.

It's such an adventure to try new things. You must make sure, of course, that your date is equally adventurous. Or you can always bring along some antacid and hope for the best.

Better than that, always have a Plan B. I remember when I picked up Jerusha at her parents' house for our first date. Her parents introduced themselves, and we started talking about what the two of us were going to do that night.

I mentioned that I was thinking of taking her to P. F. Chang's, a

Chinese restaurant in Irvine. Her parents exchanged "uh-oh" expressions. The awkward moment that followed told me I better think of something else, and quick. Luckily for me, Jerusha has since grown to like Chinese food as much as I do.

Remember that you don't have to go to a restaurant to have a creative meal. How about a picnic? I'm sure there's a park nearby. If not, set things up in your backyard or on the front lawn of your church.

As for other activities, let me start with the cheap end. You don't have to spend a ton to have a great date. I've mentioned already that one of my favorites with Jerusha is taking a walk. You might have to drive a bit to really hike, but an hour car ride is just more time to talk, right?

If you like the outdoors, look into bike riding, in-line skating, or other sports. You can kayak or canoe on many small lakes or rivers. Cross-country skiing or snowshoeing together can be fun.

My wife and I love to play board games or cards. You can include others in this activity or keep it just for two. (I have a challenge for anyone who plays Jenga: The record to beat is forty-seven levels.)

If you don't like sports or games, what about reading aloud? Jerusha and I read the first three books of the Chronicles of Narnia series aloud while we were dating. It was fun to get into the stories together.

If you can and want to spend a bit more money, look in the entertainment section of your newspaper for upcoming events. Tickets for many events are discounted significantly with your student ID.

Why go to the movies when you can see real-life actors in a play or Broadway musical? Even if you can't afford to see *Phantom of the Opera,* you can catch some great shows at local playhouses.

Most symphonies, ballets, and operas also offer discounts to students. Go for it! You may find that you enjoy something like this much more than you ever imagined you could. You'll be having an adventure and stretching your mind at the same time.

Museums are another great place for a date. Check out fine art museums and visit every time a new collection comes through. If you don't like paintings and sculpture, try natural history or science museums. With all the interactive exhibits, you're sure to have a great time.

Try searching for the unique and different when it comes to museums. In Colorado we have the Pro Rodeo Hall of Fame (yee-haw!), and in Southern California, the Museum of Tolerance. There are museums for clothes, stuffed animals, toys, cars, and almost everything you could imagine.

Of course, Jerusha and I highly recommend youth or college group events for dates. About half of our dates included the entire youth group. You may not have a lot of alone time on such an occasion, but you'll get a great price on activities such as rock climbing, laser tag, or ice-skating. Plus the two of you can hang with your friends at the same time.

While we were dating, Jerusha and I also took her eleven-year-old brother, Ian, out. Taking along your younger siblings honors both them and your parents. It also protects you from doing things you shouldn't, teaches you how your date responds to children, and provides a model of healthy dating for your brother or sister. You can't lose.

If you're more serious in your relationship, try taking dance lessons together. If you're really serious, why not consider some dates with the marriage counselor at your church?

I hope that gives you some good ideas. I'm sure if you put your mind to it you can come up with tons more. Be creative and pick places that will build great memories and encourage great conversations.

Q. Who should pay?

A. If you're taking me to lunch—you!

Seriously, this question seems to be on a lot of students' minds. Here's what I think...

I believe that a gentleman will lead, even when the bill comes. I think a gentleman should take the check as soon as the waiter drops it on the table. A gentleman won't even let her wonder about an awkward "How much do I owe?" conversation. Even if it's just grabbing coffee, he uses the opportunity to pay as a way to honor his date.

To me, male leadership means treating a lady with respect and class; and that means treating her to dinner as a way to say thank you for her company.

Many young women today are encouraged to insist on paying their own way. They're told that this shows independence and assertiveness and that if they don't pay, guys will get the wrong impression.

I hope these issues are nonexistent for you. Still, it's worth mentioning that if you pay for a date, gentlemen, that's all you did. You didn't earn the right for a second date or a good-night kiss. You had the privilege of another person's company and the honor of taking care of her for the evening.

Some young women may still insist that you let them pay for themselves. If they feel better doing that, that's up to them. If you're a young woman who feels that way, let me challenge you for a moment. Don't pay simply because you want to be "in control" or "assert your independence." Let someone else treat you if he really wants to honor you as a lady.

As the relationship becomes more serious, a young woman may decide to pay for a date now and then. She may want to thank her boyfriend in this way for all the times he's honored her. That kind of understanding between couples develops over time.

Q. Is it bad to date a lot of different people?

A. That depends. If you're wondering whether you can date a lot of different people before you get married, I think that's fine. I had lots of dates and girlfriends before I met Jerusha.

On the other hand, if you want to know whether you can date a bunch of different people at the same time, my answer would change. It's not so much a question of whether you can do it, but how it will affect you if you do.

A few things to consider:

First of all, you're a Christian. As a representative of Christ, you must consider how your actions will appear to others around you. Even if you just want to get to know a lot of people, the perception may be that you're a "player" or a flirt.

He who dies having had the most dates doesn't win any prize. In fact, if your "girl-crazy" or "boy-crazy" behavior negatively affects your witness, I would say you've lost—big time. Your witness is precious. It isn't worth the risk that someone might think you're reckless or that you have your priorities out of whack.

Consider this as well: If you have a hundred friends, they average getting only a hundredth of your time. You may have a lot of shallow relationships, but that's not the point of companionship. You can't develop close personal relationships without time, investment, and energy.

You know that some dates won't go anywhere and that some relationships are doomed to dead-end. Don't waste your time on these relationships just because you want to date as many people as possible. Be selective.

The Bible warns against the folly of maintaining too many relationships at one time: "A man of many companions may come to ruin" (Proverbs 18:24). You may come to ruin if you don't truly invest in your closest friendships. You won't be able to balance all the needs and demands of multiple relationships. Trying to keep all the plates spinning will probably drive you crazy rather than make you happy.

Invest your dating time wisely. Not only will you be less stressed, but you'll protect the feelings of others at the same time.

Q. How much time should a couple be spending together?

A. Different stages of dating allow or call for different amounts of time together, so some couples will naturally spend more time together than others.

Balance is the key.

Your relationships should always benefit and enhance your life. If you're doing worse in school because you stay up all night talking on the phone, your relationship may be out of balance. If you're consistently late to work because you want to spend every last second with your boyfriend or girlfriend, you may need to step back and reevaluate how much time you spend together.

You may want to curb how much time you spend on the phone, which could be tough (especially if you have your own phone line). Extended calls can eat up massive amounts of your time. Make sure your calls are balanced with the rest of your life. My brother David tried to help me out with this by picking up the phone every two minutes to ask if I was off yet.

In addition, don't let a relationship cause you to miss out on other important opportunities. If you're a talented artist or athlete, develop those skills as you develop your relationship. If you're on track for an academic scholarship at a great university, don't bypass that for a relationship that may end in three months. Balance all the aspects of your life.

Even more important than opportunities or activities, don't miss out on the other relationships in your life. If your family and friends suddenly become nonentities in your daily life, you're missing out on some valuable companionship. A boyfriend or girlfriend can't be everything for you.

Above all, don't miss out on developing your relationship with the Lord. Just because you had a strong walk before you started dating doesn't mean that God wants to spend any less time with you now that you have a boyfriend or girlfriend. Stay consistent with your Savior.

If you balance the time you spend on your relationship with the time you spend on other things, you'll be well-rounded and even-keeled. Then if you happen to break up, you won't have compromised your other relationships or goals.

You'll also place greater value on your time together if you don't have as much of it. You'll look forward to each moment you get to spend with each other instead of taking it for granted.

Q. When is it okay to start kissing?

A. Many may disagree, but I say wait as long as possible. The point of your dating relationships is to get to know another person. Once you enter the physical realm, you cease to focus on the other person's character. You start thinking about kissing them, rather than talking to them.

The easiest breakup I ever experienced was with a girl I'd never kissed. Although we'd dated quite a bit, we were able to break up and stay friends. We'd made a point of getting to know each other and not kissing. Once we saw that our life goals and dreams and preferences didn't mesh, we were able to move on. We weren't caught up in a physical mess.

Bottom line: Kissing awakens other desires and can lead to an out-of-control feeling. Self-control, a fruit of the Spirit, should always be your goal. If you can't kiss without spinning out of control, just wait!

Q. What touching is okay, and what touching is not?

A. In Ephesians 5:3, we're commanded to avoid "even a hint of sexual immorality." A "hint" is the slightest indication or the minutest possibility of impurity.

Any touching that causes arousal is off limits. If hugging turns you on too much, guess what? You need to stay away from that hint of sexual immorality.

One student who asked this question wanted to see an answer that was "biblically backed up." I think this person wanted a Bible verse that said, "Don't do x, y, and z, but everything else is okay."

Don't go looking for a Bible verse that says, "Don't fondle here" or "Don't touch there." The Bible gives us something way better: *Have no hint of sexual immorality!*

Don't cop out and use the excuse that the Bible isn't clear. God has spoken more clearly about sexual immorality than almost any other subject. (If you need to refresh your memory, look back at chapter 11.)

Q. How do I break up and stay friends?

A. If you date, the reality is that you'll have to break up now and then. But you don't have to go through nasty, heart-wrenching breakups. You can break up and still maintain common courtesy, if not a strong friendship.

Breaking up can actually be a healthy response to the development of a relationship. If you know things won't progress further, breaking up is the smartest thing you can do. How you break things off will determine the course of your future friendship.

Most nasty breakups focus on the negative parts of the relationship. Each person blames the other for "saying this" or "not doing that." They focus on what's wrong with each other.

Even if you squabble or fight as a relationship ends, you don't have to choose to focus on the negative. Choose instead to focus on the good memories. You can always choose to focus on the positive. Highlight all the great qualities that drew you to that person in the beginning and remember the fun times you had together. Don't replay hurtful or negative memories in your mind.

More important, maintain your focus on Christ. If your relationship focuses on Christ from the beginning, you're far more likely to avoid a nasty breakup at the end.

A relationship is like a bridge between two people. If the couple places all the weight of their relationship on the "love" they feel, and they break up later when the feelings die, the bridge will collapse and the two will resent each other.

On the other hand, if the bridge is built while focusing on Christ, the couple doesn't need to fear breaking up. If God holds the weight, He'll sustain the friendship after the relationship changes.

If you commit ahead of time to focusing your relationship on Christ, and if you focus on the positive rather than the negative, you probably won't have a problem staying friends after breaking up.

Of course, if you need some space—because you've been hurt or for some other reason—there's nothing wrong with maintaining distance while you heal. You don't have to be best friends with someone you break up with. If you choose not to, that's fine. But you must try not to let bitterness and anger overcome you. Ask Christ to take your pain. He has promised to carry all our burdens.

Even if the other person has hurt you, treat him or her with love and respect. You can never go wrong by responding in love, as Jesus would.

Q. How can I tell the difference between true love and infatuation?

A. Discerning the difference between love and infatuation can be hard for a lot of young people.

Infatuation is a great deceiver, and it often fools people into believing they're "in love" when they're really just obsessed with a counterfeit version of it.

You may be experiencing infatuation if you can't get your mind off a person or if he or she seems perfect in your eyes. When that person is around, infatuation can make you feel weak and high at the same time. And the intense emotional sensations that person awakens in you can make you feel out of control.

The tough thing is that these things may also happen when you're genuinely in love. Thank goodness there *are* ways to tell love and infatuation apart:

- Love is backed up by commitment and faithfulness, while infatuation is short-lived and fleeting.
- Love can and will work through all kinds of problems; infatuation throws in the towel.
- Love is grounded in reality. You know the person isn't perfect, but you love him or her anyway. Infatuation is more like fantasy; it overlooks all faults and puts its object on a pedestal.
- Love can let go; infatuation clings.
- Love builds up; infatuation sucks life away.

Obviously, love tops infatuation on every point. I pray that you'll learn to truly love, avoiding infatuation at all costs.

Q. What's the big deal about dating? Why all the controversy?

A. Now we've come full circle to the issues we took up in the opening pages of this book.

I believe dating is a big deal because I've seen so many young people struggle with it. There's a lot of confusion, misunderstanding, and hurt out there, and young adults want answers to their dating and relationship questions.

Dating is also a big deal because people have such strong opinions about what's right and what's not. The "no dating" movement has gained so much popularity that I felt compelled to write this book. That movement grew out of a desire to curb reckless dating. Christian leaders and parents wanted to keep their kids away from premarital sex, heartbreak, and broken curfews. Ending dating seemed the best solution.

On some college campuses, young men and women don't even spend time together anymore. They don't even try to develop relationships with the opposite sex—they think it best to avoid the other gender altogether.

One young man at a Christian college in California actually asked, "Why do I even need a girl as a friend?" That's like asking why we even need to have two genders at all! We need to learn from one another and lean on one another. For the rest of our lives we'll have to interact with both men and women, so we need to learn how to do so in a godly way.

Some young women are afraid of men, convinced that they'll be hurt. Has the opposite sex really become the enemy? As Christians we should be able to develop relationships without fear.

Others buy into the lie that men and women are really the same and that any perceived differences should be abolished. But the differences between men and women are real, and our relationships should celebrate them. "In our wise Creator's providence," Stu Weber writes in *Tender Warrior,* "these differences were intended to be pleasurable, effective, and even fun."

Dating also should be pleasurable, not fearful. It should be fun to get to know guys and girls. Dating should also be an effective way to learn to better relate to the opposite sex.

I'm not claiming here that dating is the only way to learn to interact with the other gender; I'm simply pointing out that fear and avoidance have been the undesirable outgrowths of an extreme movement against dating. We should not fear and avoid our brothers or sisters. Male-female interaction is essential to maturity and growth, and I believe dating can be one way to develop healthy relationships.

CROSSING THE VALLEY

Imagine you're on a journey, but the path ahead is blocked by a deep, densely forested valley. How will you cross it?

Two people step up to help you. One of them points out a tightrope that's strung across the top of the valley, far above the forest growth. He offers you a balancing stick and advises you to step onto the tightrope and start walking.

The other person offers you a compass, plus a map and guidebook showing several possibilities for carefully making your way right through the very heart of the forested valley.

Which offer would you accept?

God doesn't want you walking a tightrope of legalistic rules, even though the rules are intended to keep you far above the potential struggles of guy-girl relationships. Instead, He has given us directions in His great guidebook, the Bible, for forging our path step by step through the development of those relationships. In His grace, He lets us choose between many valid options.

Dating responsibly, I believe, is one of those options.

Options and risks frighten some people. Freedom can be a scary concept. It means risking failure. Freedom may mean that you mess up and have to start over again. But freedom is grace, and our Lord is the Author of grace.

Dating is a big deal because it's become an issue of freedom versus legalism. I hope that within the pages of this book you've found a way to date with grace and freedom and to God's glory.

Think It Over

For Personal Study and Group Discussion

INTRODUCTION: TO DATE OR NOT TO DATE
I Know What You're Thinking

1. What are your reasons for reading this book?
2. You've probably encountered discussions or even debate about whether Christians should or should not date. What are the strongest reasons you've encountered on both sides of this issue?
3. What questions related to dating have you heard from your friends (or asked yourself)?
4. Some Scriptures to explore: What evidence do you see in the following passages that God is the Source of the best advice in our relationships? Psalm 23:1 and 84:11; Philippians 4:19; and 1 John 4:16.

CHAPTER 1: THE DRIVE TO DATE
Nature, Love, and Especially God

1. What does this chapter teach about the source of our drive to date?

2. Why do you think love is so important for human beings?

3. As far as our human relationships go, why is it important to know that "God is love"?

4. Think about how the greatness and vastness of God's love is described in the following Bible passages. What encouragement do you find in each one? Psalms 57:10; 86:15; 100:5; 1 John 4:8-9.

5. What examples of romantic relationships have you noticed in the Bible?

6. What do you see as the most important differences between a romantic relationship and a friendship?

7. What are some of the obvious problems sin has caused in male-female relationships?

8. What inappropriate responses to romantic feelings have you noticed among people you know? How could these people have responded differently?

CHAPTER 2: ACCORDING TO WEBSTER
You Call That a Date?

1. In your own opinion, what differences do you see between dates and "just-friends" activities?

2. What problems might arise in a relationship between two people who are operating with different definitions of dating?

3. What kind of expectations do you think people should have when they go on dates?

4. How much do you appreciate clarity and honesty in a relationship with a member of the opposite sex? Explain your answer.

5. Why do you think it's important for us to avoid stress in our dating relationships?

6. What do you find in these biblical passages to help you steer clear of worry? John 14:27; Philippians 4:7-8; and Colossians 3:15.

7. If dating had become a god in someone's life, what evidence of this might you expect to see?

8. What do you think is the best definition of "a date"? How would you explain your definition to a friend?

CHAPTER 3: DATING BY WHOSE RULES?
For That Great First Impression—Think Again

1. Besides the worldly lies listed in this chapter, what other false guidelines about dating does the world dish out?

2. When it comes to relationships, in what ways could following the world's guidelines bring harm to you or others?

3. In your opinion, what's the most important way in which you can act differently from the world when it comes to dating?

4. What are some practical ways you can avoid flirting?

5. How have you seen the "follow your feelings" lie in music, movies, TV, books, or magazines? What do you think is the best strategy for keeping yourself from being negatively influenced by this philosophy?

6. Why is it important not to mix God's standards with worldly standards? Use Romans 12:2 to help you answer.

7. Why is it important to test every opinion against the Word of God? Look at Acts 17:11 for a biblical example of this.

8. Why do you think so many people are attracted to a legalistic approach to life?

9. What does God's grace set us free to do? See Romans 6:18-22 and Galatians 5:13 for help.

10. How would you define what it means to have "freedom in Christ"?

11. How can you use your freedom in Christ to act responsibly when it comes to dating?

CHAPTER 4: CHOOSING YOUR DATE
First Things First

1. How would you describe your own criteria for choosing a person to date?

2. Why is it wrong to date someone just because you want a relationship?

3. Think again about the two commandments that comprise God's ultimate standard, as taught by Jesus in Matthew 22:37-40. Why does loving God come before loving others?

4. What reasons for obeying God do you find in these passages? Psalm 19:7-11 and 103:17-18; Matthew 7:24-27; and 1 John 3:21-22.

5. How can a right relationship with the Lord help your other relationships?

6. How does your obedience tell God that you love Him?

7. Why would dating a nonbeliever grieve God?

8. How could dating a nonbeliever harm you? How could it harm the other person?

9. Describe any examples you've seen of people straying from God because of their relationships with non-Christians.

10. Are you willing to make a serious commitment to date only Christians? If not, why? If so, how would you graciously decline a date with a nonbeliever?

11. If you had a Christian friend who was dating a nonbeliever, what reasons would you give your friend for ending that relationship?

CHAPTER 5: RELATIONSHIP INTERVIEWS
Getting Personal

1. From what you see in this chapter, what are the advantages of thinking of a date as a "relationship interview"? And how can this perspective help you get to know a person better?

2. Why is it helpful to find out sooner rather than later that someone is not a match for you?

3. What kind of questions could you ask a date to get to know him or her better? Think of as many questions as you can.

4. This chapter emphasizes the need to simply *be yourself* in a dating situation. How can each of the following passages help you be comfortable with who you really are? Psalm 139:13-16; 2 Corinthians 5:17; Galatians 2:20; Ephesians 2:10 and 4:22-25; and 1 Peter 4:10.

5. How can you honor God in planning your dates?

6. This chapter suggests that you picture yourself running in a race and suddenly finding someone else running beside you

at the same pace and in the same direction. How would you describe someone who has your same pace and direction?

7. How can you find out more about a person's other relationships?

8. When you are on a date, what topics of conversation might affect your actions and expectations?

9. How can sticking to a curfew help you honor God while dating?

10. What three guidelines does this chapter give for determining where your date will take place? Why is each guideline important?

11. Make a list of places in your city that would be good for potential dates.

12. Why is it important to encourage the person you're dating? What's the difference between simply *complimenting* someone and truly *encouraging* that person?

13. How would you define a "predecision," as this term is presented in this chapter?

14. What are the most important predecisions you can make now about how to conduct yourself on a date?

CHAPTER 6: QUALITY CONTROL
Someday My Prince (or Princess) Will Come

1. What kind of people does your lifestyle attract today?

2. What kind of person do you believe God wants you to attract?

3. According to what you see in this chapter, what does it take to build one's character?

4. What insights do you gain from these passages about God's

methods for developing character in our lives? John 15:1-5; Romans 5:1-5; James 1:2-4; and 2 Peter 1:3-11.

5. In the story of the barbarian and the princess, imagine that the barbarian had changed his lifestyle only to "get the girl." Do you think his new lifestyle would have lasted? Why or why not?

6. Do you really believe it's important for you to build spiritual character before pursuing dating relationships? Why or why not?

7. Take a moment to answer all four of the Spiritual Inventory questions from this chapter:

> *Are you growing in the knowledge of God's truth?*
> *Are you growing as a man or woman of prayer?*
> *Are you in fellowship with other believers?*
> *Are you pursuing God's kingdom above all else?*

8. In which of these four areas do you need the most work?

9. How could you begin this week to improve in this area?

10. When it comes to character building, what long-term goal would you set for yourself?

11. How did Rebekah prepare herself to attract a man of character?

12. What do character development and relationship development have in common?

13. Why is the "instant relationship" a myth?

14. How could relationship development be hindered by daydreaming about your "prince" or "princess" coming someday?

CHAPTER 7: TIMING IS EVERYTHING
Ready...or Not?

1. What does this chapter title mean to you?
2. According to these passages, what's involved in waiting for God's perfect timing? Psalms 33:20-21; 40:1 and 130:5-6; Romans 8:25.
3. Why can we trust that God's timing is perfect? Use these passages for help in answering this question: Psalms 103:19 and 145:17-19; Isaiah 30:18; 46:9-10; and 64:4; Lamentations 3:22-23.
4. What are the three stages of "readiness" for dating as taught in this chapter?
5. What are the most important reasons for not dating until your parents allow you to?
6. Explain to what extent you agree with this statement: *The high-school years are an inappropriate time for "live or die" serious dating relationships.*
7. Have you observed any couples who got too serious, too soon? If so, what happened in their relationship?
8. What are some practical ways you can be appropriately cautious when developing your relationships?
9. Spend enough time to give thoughtful answers to these six questions concerning your readiness for a serious relationship:
   How content are you in your relationship with Christ?
   What is your motivation for a more serious relationship?
   How well have you pursued your personal spiritual growth?
   Have you set physical and emotional boundaries for this relationship?

> *Would others say you're ready?*
>
> *Do you have time for a serious relationship?*

10. From these six questions, what conclusions would you make about your readiness for a serious relationship?

11. In the following verses, what examples does God give us for how to rely on *His* love rather than on a dating relationship? Psalm 13:5-6; 16:2; 17:6-8; 18:1-3; and 63:1-5.

CHAPTER 8: COMPROMISING WHO YOU ARE FOR WHAT YOU WANT

Mediocrity Versus Excellence

1. For what reasons would a Christian choose to compromise his faith and relationship to God by dating a nonbeliever? What makes these reasons seem so strong?

2. As you understand it, how does the Enemy deceive and tempt committed believers?

3. Why is it essential that we look at our present dating life with the future in mind?

4. What's the most important lesson you learn from Samson's story?

5. What happens to people who settle for mediocrity instead of staying committed to excellence? Think of an example from your life or someone else's that demonstrates the destructive force of compromise.

6. According to what the following passages teach, what can you rely on to help you stay alert to temptation and committed to excellence? 1 Corinthians 10:13; Philippians 4:8; Hebrews 13:20-21; James 4:7-8; and 2 Peter 1:3-4.

7. How is it possible to compromise in a relationship even if the person you're dating is a Christian?

8. What are some practical ways that Christians can "stay alert" in their dating relationships?

9. How are complacency and pride harmful to your spiritual health?

10. Whenever you're tempted to compromise, how can you handle it the way Joseph did in the Bible?

CHAPTER 9: DEFENDING THE EMOTIONAL ZONE
Guarding Your Heart

1. Why do we crave intimacy with others?

2. What things characterize relationships that are emotionally intimate?

3. Why is it wrong to expect humans to meet our need for intimacy?

4. Why is it right to seek emotional intimacy with God before seeking emotional intimacy in a dating relationship?

5. For a superstrong foundation in experiencing intimacy with God, explore any of the following passages to see what they communicate about God's intensely personal and emotional involvement with His sons and daughters—including you! Psalms 147:11 and 149:4-5; Isaiah 41:10; Jeremiah 31:3; Zephaniah 3:17; John 1:12-13 and 3:16-17; Romans 8:28-29; Ephesians 1:3-6; 1 John 3:1-2; Revelation 21:1-4.

6. How would you define the term "emotional boundary"?

7. How would you explain the difference between having emotional boundaries and refusing to get close to anyone?

8. Look at the five reasons given in this chapter for why you need emotional boundaries. Which one of these reasons motivates you the most?

9. Why is it important to set boundaries before you go on a date or begin a dating relationship?

10. What topics do you know you want to avoid in your conversation during a date?

11. How would you explain your emotional boundaries to someone else?

12. How can having emotional boundaries improve your relationships?

13. How can having emotional boundaries in these relationships strengthen your walk with God?

CHAPTER 10: GETTING AHEAD OF YOURSELF
Did Somebody Say "Marriage"?

1. Think about the three unbalanced dating approaches discussed in this chapter: How does each involve breaking healthy emotional boundaries? And in what ways can they cause a person to be selfish and shallow in his or her relationships?

2. How would you explain the difference between how singles and married couples should act?

3. What's the secret to knowing God's will, as taught in this chapter?

4. How closely is your life lined up with God's will in each of the following five major areas (as quoted from John MacArthur's book):

That you be saved.

That you be filled with God's Spirit through studying His Word.

That you be pure—sanctified and holy.

That you be obedient.

That you be humble, even in suffering.

5. What principles in each of these passages can help you grow in understanding God's will for your life? Psalm 23:3 and 32:8; Proverbs 3:5-6; Romans 8:26-27 and 12:2; and 1 Thessalonians 4:3 and 5:16-18.

6. What are the most important ways you can focus your dating relationships to help you *be* the right person instead of *finding* the right person?

7. What kind of qualities and traits should you be looking for in a person you would choose to date? And in what ways (if any) does this list differ from the list of qualities and traits you should be looking for in a person you would choose to marry?

CHAPTER 11: THE PHYSICAL FENCE
How Far Is Too Far?

1. Explain to what extent you agree with this statement: The Christian life isn't about living as close as possible to the edge of immorality; it's about living as close as possible to Jesus Christ.

2. When it comes to the physical side of a dating relationship, why is "How far is too far?" the wrong question?

3. From what you saw in this chapter, what does the Greek word *porneia* mean in the Bible?

4. In your own Bible, read 1 Corinthians 6:15–7:2 (the same passage that this chapter focused on). Summarize all the reasons Paul gives there for avoiding sexual immorality.

5. How could premature physical intimacy harm you both now and later?

6. How can setting and staying within physical boundaries protect you from the world?

7. What kinds of things can "set you off" physically?

8. Why is it important to guard your mind and eyes as much as your body?

9. According to 1 Corinthians 6:18, what does God tell us to do when we're faced with sexual temptation?

10. How can you find help in the battle for purity by planning ahead of time what you'll do on a date and where you'll go?

11. Why is it important to set and uphold your own physical boundaries?

12. According to this chapter, what is "the most important strategy in your war to remain pure"?

13. What principles and promises in the following passages can help you rely on God's strength when you face temptation? Proverbs 14:27; Romans 6:14; 1 Corinthians 10:12-13; Hebrews 2:18 and 4:14-16; James 1:13-17 and 4:7.

14. Have you ever gone farther sexually than you would have liked? If so, have you prayed for God's forgiveness? How can you plan for purity in this area in the future?

15. Once you've set your physical boundaries, how would you respond to someone who told you they were too narrow?

16. "How pure can I be?"—what is your answer to that question?

17. When it comes to taking your stand either for purity or for pleasure, what is your commitment before God?

CHAPTER 12: LIVING IN THE LIGHT
Finding Help in Accountability Partnerships

1. How would you explain what it means to live your life in God's light? And what are some practical ways to do this?
2. What are some potential dangers and downsides to sneaking around in relationships?
3. In your dating experience, is there anyone you have deceived and with whom you now need to reconcile?
4. How does placing your family's good above your own good honor God as well as your family?
5. If your parents are not believers or haven't given you the wisest counsel about dating, to which older Christians can you turn for advice and guidance?
6. How has God used a Christian friend to help reveal your blind spots?
7. Which friends could help keep you on your toes when it comes to godly dating?
8. Why is it necessary to be consistent and specific when you meet together with someone for accountability?
9. In your own opinion (or from what you've seen in this chapter), what other factors contribute to successful accountability?
10. Why do you think friendship accountability can be one of the greatest aspects of Christian fellowship? Look at these Scriptures to help you shape your answer: Proverbs 17:17; 18:24; and 27:17; Matthew 18:19-20; Galatians 6:2; Hebrews 10:24-25; and 1 John 1:5-7.

CHAPTER 13: JUST FOR GIRLS, JUST FOR GUYS
A Closer Focus

For the Guys:

1. Why is it wrong to lead a girl "into the jungle"?
2. What kind of problems might arise in "leading a girl on"?
3. From what you see in this chapter (and from what you've learned in the Bible), what does God want from you as a man?
4. What position has God given you as a man?
5. What skills has God given you that can help you be a leader?
6. Of the men you know, who do you most respect? How does he treat the women around him?
7. What is the proper way to "be serious" about every relationship?
8. How should a man treat his mother and sisters? Should he treat a date better, worse, or the same?
9. Have you ever been in a bad situation in which you and your date were struggling to maintain your physical boundaries? What happened? How could you have been a better leader in that situation?
10. In this chapter I mentioned the top five things to avoid in a relationship—obsession, jealous rages, fear, the love-hate cycle, and out-of-control physicality. Which of these five are you most likely to struggle with? And in what practical ways can you fight that tendency?
11. What definition for *pornography* is given in this chapter? What influences in your life fall under this definition?
12. What can you do to remove these influences? Are you willing to do it? If removing the influence isn't possible, what

can you do to lessen its pressure or to avoid the lust it causes?

13. Are you willing to ask for help and accountability in the battle against pornography? Who is one man you could trust to guide and counsel you in this area?

For the Girls:

1. How would you define flirtatious behavior?
2. How can flirting harm others? How can it harm you?
3. Why is modesty a sensitive issue for women today?
4. How does being modest or immodest reflect on your character?
5. Why is modesty about more than clothing?
6. Of the women you know, which ones do you most respect? Why do you respect them? Do the most respectable women tend to dress modestly or immodestly?
7. How can an immodest woman be "obtrusive" or "in someone's way"?
8. What clothes do you own that reveal more of you than God wants you to reveal?
9. What does it mean to you that women were created by God to "respond"?
10. In my answer to the girls' question "Why do I never get asked out?" I described four types of girls. Which of these four are you most like? Why is it important to strive to be like the fourth woman?
11. Have you observed a situation in which someone said yes to a date just to avoid hurting the guy's feelings? What happened? What potential problems could arise from saying yes to a date when you aren't really interested?

12. If someone pushes you beyond your physical boundaries, what should you do? Why do you need to communicate firmly and vocally?

13. Have you ever had to say "no" to someone who wanted more physically? What happened? How could you have avoided that situation altogether?

CHAPTER 14: INQUIRING MINDS WANT TO KNOW
More Questions...and Answers

1. What other ideas can you think of for dates that are fun and adventurous (and affordable)?

2. When is it right for a guy to pay for a date? When would it be appropriate for the girl to pay?

3. Do you think a person can maintain more than one romantic relationship at the same time without bringing harm to himself or others? Why or why not? Have you seen others try to do this? If so, how healthy were the relationships?

4. How can balancing your dating relationships benefit your entire life?

5. How well-balanced are you in the amount of time and energy you devote to dating? Do you need to make some adjustments? If so, how can you put those changes into effect right away?

6. Why do you think it would be easier to maintain a healthy dating relationship if you hold off on kissing?

7. What are some practical ways to focus a dating relationship on Christ instead of on the other person?

8. Can you spot the difference between love and infatuation? How is infatuation inferior to genuine love?

9. If someone told you that dating is sinful, how would you respond?

10. What other questions about dating come to your mind after reading this book?

11. In your opinion, what are the most important concepts and ideas presented in this book? In what ways, if any, has reading this book changed your thinking about dating?

12. How would you summarize *in practical terms* the guidelines for godly relationships that the Lord gives in the following passages? How does each guideline support the concepts and issues we've discussed? Romans 12:9-10; Galatians 6:9-10; Colossians 3:12-14; and 1 Peter 1:22.

13. In what ways will your life be different because you've read this book?

Acknowledgments

Lord, thank You for this wonderful opportunity. You have given more than I could have ever hoped for. Your grace has blessed every part of my life; I love You.

To Jerusha, my wife of noble character: You are the woman of my dreams and my song of joy. Your love shelters me and gives me passion for tomorrow. Your eloquence and your total involvement with this book gave my dull words life. We wrote this as one.

I am indebted to Doug Gabbert and Thomas Womack for their encouragement as this project took shape. You challenge me to be more than I am…especially when Dr. Pain is present.

Thanks to all those who read and commented on the "work in progress." To Brian Aaby, my biggest help in this arduous task: At least it gave us an excuse to talk for hours. You are a true friend. To Adam Dorband, who will make a great youth pastor someday. To Dean Walton: Your perspective as a parent was invaluable. And to Melanie Edwards, whose intelligence and clear thinking I admire greatly.

I would like to acknowledge each of my mentors in the faith. Eric Heard, who I am proud to have worked with for four years: No matter how busy you were, you always had time for me. Your example gave me something to strive for. Doug Haag, who discipled me faithfully for three years: I miss Mondays at Millie's. Your strength and wisdom continue to guide me. John Fairchild, who trained me at Rocky Peak and let me live in his garage: "How hot is that door?" Dr. Phillip Howard, whose love for God's Word and commitment to prayer inspire me: Valley Bible will always be my home church. And Ted Montoya, my "Paul": You called me out to be a man of God. You took me under your wing and taught me how to fly.

I would also like to express my deepest gratitude and affection to "The Crew," the men who have kept me accountable and supported me in every way: Anthony Naimo, you are my closest friend and my "best man." I am blessed to have a friend as faithful as you. Brian Aaby, thanks for your example in ministry and in marriage. Darryl Goltiao, thanks for being open and honest, strong and consistent with Christ.

To my partners in youth ministry "crime": Tim "Semper Fi" Coulombe, Matt "I'm gonna kill you" Coulombe, Billy Tarka, and Jeff Tacklind—may God continue to bless your ministries.

Carl, you know who you are.

To all the students and leaders of EV Free Fullerton's Class of 1998: Thank you for four unforgettable years. To "The Boyz"—Arie Barendrecht, Scott Belon, Phil Girod, Tom Haag, Paul Heimlich, Jesse LaTour, Matt Mittelman, Mike Sailhamer, Chad Staffieri, and Matt Thompson: You helped me be a better leader. "C'mon Phil, real quick!"

Thank you to "my youth group" at Tri-Lakes Chapel and to the entire church body for your love and support.

And finally, to my brother David: I am proud of the man of God you have become. I admire your dedication to Denise, Chase, and Emilee. You are more than a brother; you are a friend.

Can't-miss insight into girl guy relationships.

You *can* have well-defined, emotionally safe, and rewarding dating relationships that honor God! Find everything you need to know about pursuing healthy dating relationships that are characterized by holiness and integrity.

"Jeramy and Jerusha address things such as good communication skills, how to guard emotional as well as sexual purity, and what it means to have a God-centered self."

—DR. LORI SALIERNO, speaker and author

"A balanced, entertaining, and biblically oriented overview of this critical issue."

—DENNIS RAINEY, executive director of FamilyLife